THE
CALL UP

THE
CALL UP

A STUDY OF NATIONAL SERVICE
IN PEACETIME BRITAIN

PHIL CARRADICE

FONTHILL

Fonthill Media Language Policy

Fonthill Media publishes in the international English language market. One language edition is published worldwide. As there are minor differences in spelling and presentation, especially with regard to American English and British English, a policy is necessary to define which form of English to use. The Fonthill Policy is to use the form of English native to the author. Phil Carradice was born and educated in Wales; therefore British English has been adopted in this publication.

Fonthill Media Limited
Fonthill Media LLC
www.fonthillmedia.com
office@fonthillmedia.com

First published in the United Kingdom and the United States of America 2016

British Library Cataloguing in Publication Data:
A catalogue record for this book is available from the British Library

ISBN 978-1-78155-526-2

Typeset in 10.5pt on 13pt Minion Pro
Printed and bound by CPI Group (UK) Ltd, Croydon, CR0 4YY

Acknowledgements

First and foremost, grateful thanks to the men who happily and willingly recounted their experiences of national service life. Without their memories, this book would not have been possible.

Thanks also to the men of the Merchant Navy, who told their stories about serving at sea as an alternative to national service—often an overlooked and neglected area.

Thanks to all those men and women who spoke to me about deferred service—miners, agricultural workers, students, and the rest.

Huge thanks to John Morris, who willingly and brilliantly produced drawings of several ships on which national servicemen sailed. Your skill is equalled only by your generosity.

Thanks to the staff of Cardiff Central Library, informative and efficient as ever.

Thanks to the editors of *Sea Breezes*, *The Western Mail*, and the *Barry/Cowbridge/Llantwit Major Gem*, who happily published letters from me asking for help in the project.

Finally, thanks to Trudy, my wife—your support, as ever, has been invaluable.

CONTENTS

Introduction

Peacetime conscription in Britain existed for just sixteen years, from 1947 until 7 May 1963, when Private Fred Turner of the Army Catering Corps, the last conscript, was returned to civilian life. Yet its effects are still remembered and felt by the men—young at the time, but now old—who were forced to endure their prescribed two years of military service in the Army, Navy, or RAF. They may not have enjoyed the experience at the time, but many now look back reasonably fondly—and, perhaps, with a modicum or two of rose-tinted memories of the past—at a period that, in the parlance of the time, 'made a man of them'.

> Two years of hard military discipline, backed up by a brutality that shocked, offended and, to be honest, seriously damaged some, was out of the experience of so many of the conscripts. And the most depressing thing about the whole process was that they simply had no choice. In the words of one national serviceman: 'I always had the feeling of involuntary slavery with petty dictators parading around making life unbearable and miserable for everyone'.
>
> Reg Jones (RAF)

Yet, despite the drawbacks, despite the pain and anguish, despite that feeling of 'slavery', national service gave young men experiences they could never have dreamed about. From the harsh realities of jungle warfare to the glories of South Sea Islands, from the unmitigated boredom of huge Army camps to the welcoming warmth of the NAAFI, they saw and endured it all. Hindsight might well play a part, but a constant theme from the memories of the men who served seems to be 'I'm glad I did it'.

> Enjoyment—if, indeed, enjoyment it was—came slowly. 'Before you went in there was trepidation but after six months you felt as if you'd been there all your life—great camaraderie, great friends'.
>
> Alun Williams (RAF)

Sadly there are no soldiers alive now from the First World War, and fairly soon there will be none from the Second World War either. It will not be too long before the men who were called up for national service will also be gone. That is why they deserve to be remembered.

This book focuses directly on the experiences of the men, using their words and their memories—backed up by some wonderful and atmospheric photographs that catch fleeting impressions of a world out of time. I have tried to keep observations and judgements to a minimum. It is up to the reader to form opinions and views, based on the words of the men who were there at the time.

National service conscripts—this is their story.

Phil Carradice
St Athan, 2015

The Call Up

On 2 September 1945, in a formal ceremony held on the deck of the US battleship *Missouri*, the American Supreme Commander in the Pacific, General Douglas MacArthur, oversaw the surrender of all Japanese military forces. It was a moment of spectacular anti-climax, the dropping of atomic bombs on Hiroshima and Nagasaki only the month before having effectively driven the Empire of Japan to its knees. However punitive or painful it might have been for the defeated Japanese, however joyful for the Allies, the ceremony neatly brought the Second World War to a close.

The war in Europe had already ended four months before and MacArthur's signature on the surrender document was little more than the last rites in a conflict that had lasted for six years and a day, had affected more than 200 nations, and caused well over 50 million casualties.

For the soldiers of all nations, defeated and victorious alike, the priority now was to get home and back to civilian life as quickly and as easily as possible. In the United Kingdom, the demobilisation of troops—demob as it was commonly called—was nothing short of frenetic.

Between October 1945 and October 1946, over 100,000 men and women were discharged from the forces. Strangely, even as that vast number of soldiers were being released, because conscription had not yet ended and there were jobs to be done in the recently liberated territories, men under the age of thirty were still being called up to serve their country—a clear case of the government giving with one hand and taking back with the other.[1]

The rationale for continuing with conscription was simple. Despite the effect of the war upon her standing in world affairs, despite her crippled finances and economy, Britain was still a colonial power, one with significant responsibilities in various parts of the world. It would need large numbers of personnel to carry out the tasks required, in what was now a very different, post-war world; to the members of the newly elected Labour Government, there seemed to be just one answer—national service.

Extending wartime conscription was one thing, introducing peacetime enlistment (a process that might well last for a decade or more) was rather different. From the outset, it was clear that demands on the declining British Empire would be enormous:

It is calculated that to meet the production and related requirements of the Services during the financial year 1947–48 that a labour force of about 450,000 will be needed.[2]

National service in peacetime, the enforced enlistment of young men into the Army, Navy, and RAF was, at best, a 'knee-jerk' reaction to a potential problem, a way of re-establishing the status quo for politicians who had been brought up on the dream of Empire. At first, Prime Minister Attlee was not sure, but Ernest Bevin, the man who had been in charge of wartime conscription, was adamant. Using the argument that conscription would help to make a more democratic Britain, he managed to sell the idea to the trade unions and to the country as a whole.

In the early post-war days, there was little thought that countries like Malaya, Kenya, or Cyprus would ever want to stand apart from 'the mother country', and the role of hastily trained conscripts was simply to re-establish order and routine. It was to be, effectively, a job of policing people and countries that had been thrown into chaos by the war and now needed a little stability that could only be provided by firm but fair paternal control.

In the inevitable post-war confusion following a conflict that had decimated people and countries across the globe, by 1946, unrest was already beginning to consume many of Britain's colonial possessions. Very few of those in power saw the rumblings and resentments for what they really were—the first pangs of a growing thirst for independence.

As for national service, in the eyes of many, it was nothing more than an extension of wartime conscription. The only difference was that now the young men who were called up to serve in the forces would not be required to fight against German and Japanese soldiers, merely the Nationalists in each country.

Debate about the idea of peacetime conscription raged, in parliament and in the country as a whole, for some time. Even the Labour Party, which was proposing the measure, was split:

> Following a visit to Pwllheli by Mr Rhys Davies, Socialist MP, in his campaign against military conscription in time of peace, a meeting of representatives of all denominations, held at Pwllheli on Saturday, planned a series of meetings in every town and village in the Lleyn Peninsula for protest against conscription.[3]

Future Prime Minister Jim Callaghan, Chair of the Defence and Services Committee of the Parliamentary Labour Party—thirty-three of them being ex-servicemen—lent his support to the fifty-plus members of the party who had already come out as being opposed to the idea. Callaghan did eventually agree to support the government, but only on the condition that certain stipulations would be met. Even Winston Churchill was not totally in favour of the plan:

> Call up at 21 seemed very severe even though the Army was a very different business now from what it was in the days when a red coat was not allowed inside a public house and was treated as the scum of the population—until a war broke out.[4]

Whatever the opinions of politicians and newspapers, there remained an element of paternalism in the air, even with the socialist members of the new government. Now convinced that the cheapest and safest way to ensure stability in the world (for Britain, at least) was through a process of national service, Prime Minister Clement Attlee was quite happy to tell his cabinet that he did not think a period of service in the armed forces was an unreasonable return for the creation of the new Welfare State.[5] It was an attitude shared by many.

After much heated debate, the 1948 National Service Act came into force on 1 January 1949 and was just one element in what was later seen as a revolutionary period in British politics. Mines and railways were nationalised, a new educational system was introduced, and the National Health Service, with all its many faults, was created. A period of enforced military service might seem out of place with such 'good works', but it must be viewed in the context of the time, in a country that had resolutely fought for freedom from oppression for several years. As such, it was the product of a people or a nation who did not want to be caught unaware or unready ever again.

It was hardly surprising that, by 1950, national servicemen made up half the strength of the British Army. Before the call up was ended in 1963, '2.5 million young men were compelled to do their national service—with 6,000 being called up every fortnight'.[6] The downside to this was that voluntary enlistment dropped sharply, but, while there were national servicemen to fill the gaps, it was not something that unduly concerned military planners.

The Army was always the major employer of national servicemen. Out of every 100 recruits the Navy took only two, the RAF took thirty, and the Army absorbed the rest. Such a displacement was perhaps inevitable, not so much because of the technical demands that the Navy and RAF made on servicemen, but because of the huge numbers of support staff required to keep a modern army in the field.

By the terms of the act, all healthy males between the ages of eighteen and twenty-one would be liable for service in the armed forces for a period of eighteen months. It would be followed by a period of four years in reserve. The message to the youth of the country was simple and was outlined in a very basic, almost brutal communication that everyone received once they had been passed fit by a medical board:

> In accordance with the National Service Act 1948.... you are called up for service in the Regular Army (or Navy or Air Force) and are required to present yourself etc., etc.

The date, time, and barracks or base where the recruit was required to present himself were outlined in the same letter. The length of service varied over the years, at one stage a shortened period of just one year being suggested, but it began with the period set at eighteen months. With the outbreak and expansion of the Korean War in 1950–51, however, national service was revised to a slightly longer two years and there it remained until the end of the system in 1963.

The period in reserve was, in the minds of many, the most important part of the process. Within months of the war ending, Winston Churchill's Iron Curtain had descended across Europe and, in the late 1940s, the threat posed by Stalin's Russia was both real and terrifying. Should war come, it was crucial that Britain could call on soldiers who were trained and experienced. On demob, every soldier was issued with a General Reservists Instruction Book:

> This book is issued for information and guidance to all men who, being members of the Army General Reserve by virtue of the Navy, Army and Air Force Reserves Acts … have been selected by the competent military authority for IMMEDIATE recall to military service in the event of a NATIONAL EMERGENCY.[7]

The capital letters were the governments, but they served to emphasise the importance of the reservists in the days before the threat of nuclear war made infantry assault virtually obsolete. Initially popular, particularly with those who would not have to serve, it was not long before the concept of enforced enlistment began to pall.

For sixteen years—although the last three were little more than a winding down period when few were called and even fewer chosen—the thought and threat of national service hung over the youth of Britain like a modern-day sword of Damocles. In an age of post-war austerity, the idea of two years of national service did not lie easily on the consciousness of the young. It was the time of teenage rebellion, of teddy boys and motorbike gangs, and of coffee bars and rock and roll. Compulsory service and the discipline imposed by the military were, to many young men, unpalatable in the extreme.

Stories of mindless bullying by NCOs and the dark days of basic training might have been exaggerated or even apocryphal, but to the young would-be recruits they were terrifying. The peacetime Army, in particular, seemed to be a hide-bound nineteenth-century organisation, where tradition and regimental honour were far more important than the care of recruits. For many of the more analytically minded national servicemen, people like the novelist David Lodge, the Army of post-war Britain was an anachronism that simply continued the iniquities of the past:

> …the peacetime Army, where the rigid demarcation between officers, sergeants and other ranks was based on, and preserved, the class distinctions of pre-war British society.[8]

Whatever its faults, whatever its problems, national service lasted from 1947 until 1963. Britain had previously only instigated conscription in time of war—during the First World War, from 1916–1918, and from 1939 for the duration of the Second World War. Peacetime conscription, therefore, was a unique social phenomenon in Britain and its effect on the men who endured it has been lasting.

Since the end of the system in 1963, there have often been calls to reinstate national service—from ex-servicemen, from harassed parents, from the media, and even from those charged with a duty to uphold law and order; 'it made a man of me' is often the cry, 'it will do the same to the feckless youth of today'. There might be an element of truth in this, but the tendency to be reactive in the face of social problems is not a new phenomenon, as researchers investigating the mods and rockers battles of the 1960s at seaside resorts like Brighton and Margate quickly found out:

> Many of those interviewed thought that magistrates should be able to order the birching of young offenders; others called for the return of National Service, a common theme in the sixties—even though the rise in juvenile crime had started long before it was abolished.[9]

Bringing back national service has never really been an option. To begin with, the reason for its creation in the first place—to police and manage the outposts of empire—has long since vanished. Additionally, modern weapons of war, whichever service you look at, require far more expertise than can ever be acquired after a few weeks of basic training.

Most people who demand a return of national service do so thinking that its stringencies and rigid acceptance of discipline would be good for the development of young people. However, in order for the old system to work, there would have to be automatic responses to what were often mindless orders. It was a system backed up by the brutality of the parade ground and barrack room, a system invariably controlled (at least at the basic training stage) by petty tyrants, whose status depended on their own idiosyncratic whims.

The world has changed and people these days simply would not accept the dictates and the punishments that were regularly meted out in the 1940s and 1950s. As such, any attempt to reintroduce conscription—for whatever reason—would be counterproductive. Yet, national service undoubtedly brought self-awareness and self-control to many. These days it is difficult to find a national servicemen who does not look back fondly on his time in the armed forces. Rose-tinted spectacles they might be, but there is no denying the genuine strength of feeling contained in the memories of these men.

> I can honestly say that I enjoyed my national service. It gave me discipline and helped me to stand on my own two feet. I suppose it helped that my brothers and I weren't particularly close. I can't say I went home very often, but one month, for some reason, I was back there three times. My brother said, 'If you're going to come home that often you'll have you pay a bit more than the 10 shillings the RAF sends now.' That did it, I stayed on base.
>
> Yes I enjoyed my time in the RAF. I don't think they got a lot out of me, but I certainly got a lot out of them.
>
> Alun Williams (RAF)

> The experience and the discipline were amazing. My time in the Army instilled in me a degree of discipline that has served me well all my life. I know it's a cliché, but there are lots of youngsters out there now who could do with something like it.
>
> Derek Grattidge (Army: Horse Guards)

I really enjoyed my time in the Navy. I went in as a boy and came out as a man. It certainly hardened me up, prepared me for life. I don't know if it would work now, but my time in the Navy gave me a chance to see the world and meet so many different people.

Jim Clarke (Navy)

I enjoyed my time in the RAF and saw lots of places I'd never, normally, have got to. But should national service be reinstated? Absolutely not. Why subject millions of pleasant young men to the stupidity of square bashing and the total disruption of their lives. If we are trying to stamp out hooliganism, let the education and court systems handle it.

Reg Jones (RAF)

National service was, for many, an unwelcome imposition to both careers and life style. For me, it changed my life, from a pimply immature teenager to a self-confident, disciplined, and socially aware young man. As I now reflect, almost sixty years on, those years and the life experiences the Royal Navy gave me carried a legacy that helped me to achieve a successful corporate career. And for that I am most grateful.

Trevor Pickering (Navy)

While many men gained immeasurably from their time in the armed forces, there were also many who could not cope and were damaged, physically and emotionally, by their experiences. The story of pop singer Terry Dene, who had a huge popular hit with 'A White Sport Coat' at the end of the 1950s, is well known. Unable to cope with the pressures and the bullying, he had a nervous breakdown and was discharged from the Army after just two weeks. His singing career never recovered.

Tragically, there were suicides, men driven beyond their limits, but able to see no way out of their dilemma. However, there seem to be no formal records of suicide numbers as many commanding officers quietly attributed such deaths to accident rather than design. Estimates vary, but the instances of suicide were probably in the region of nine or ten each year.[10] David Lodge's account of one man driven too far and 'back-squadded' by his NCO—sent back to complete basic training again—might be a work of fiction, but there can be no denying that the emotions and the fear he describes are totally accurate:

We found Percy behind the foetid latrine, lying on his rifle, a horrible stain creeping swiftly through the turf around his body.... He made no sound, but his eyes bulged from their sockets, as if he were astonished by so much pain.[11]

Suicide notes were rare, if not non-existent. That does not mean the act of taking their own lives was an impulsive, unconsidered action by the men concerned. Such a drastic step would have been turning over and over in a man's mind for weeks; while many of the tales about suicide and death were undoubtedly apocryphal (rumours spreading from one barracks hut to the next like jungle wild fire), when the recruits encountered it, sudden death made an immediate impact:

> A tragic incident happened very shortly after arrival. A young lad in the next billet, from the draft before ours, hanged himself at night in the billet. I understand he had been accused of stealing. We were all hurriedly called into the gym hall and addressed by the CO, telling us that if we had any issues, personal or otherwise, we were to speak to an officer or an NCO. But for some, of course, that wasn't easy.
>
> Bev Steele (Army)

A few months later, now stationed in Germany with the BAOR, Bev Steele once again encountered sudden and unexpected death. This time it was events back home that caused the problem:

> Back in Germany, things occasionally got a bit frayed and we had another tragedy. One of the fellows from our neighbouring troop shot himself when on guard, having, we later learned, received a 'Dear John' letter from his wife.
>
> Bev Steele (Army)

Suicide and discharge on medical grounds were rare. Most men just lowered their heads and tried to ignore the more disagreeable aspects of national service, while enjoying the bits that were pleasant and reassuring—the comradeship, the experience of exotic places, and the warm glow that came from the success of a job well done. Sometimes, of course, the 'powers that be' got it wrong and called up men who were clearly meant for other tasks:

> In the late '40s I was mate on a Thames sailing barge, sailing out of Faversham. Because we sometimes dipped our bow into the North Sea I was classified as a merchant seaman and was, therefore, exempt from national service as long as I stayed at sea until I was twenty-six. That wasn't why I worked on the barges, it was family tradition and I never thought of it as a way of avoiding the call up.
>
> But then, in mid-1949, I changed barges and that meant coming ashore for a few weeks while the new barge was made ready. Would you believe it, I received my call-up papers.
>
> I suppose I could have protested, but barge work was hard—all that nonsense about Thames barges being crewed by one man and a boy is exactly that, nonsense. So I just accepted it and, in January 1950, went into the Army Catering Corps.
>
> John Cotton (Army)

For Reg Jones, it was not a mistake that took him into the forces, it was a deliberate action on his part, despite having been given a five-year deferment in order to complete his apprenticeship. He knew that he would have to do his national service—or an acceptable alternative—at some stage in the future, but, by allowing that deferment to lapse and then going into the RAF, he pre-empted the process. It was a considered and conscious act:

> In September 1951, I began a five-year apprenticeship with Cammell Lairds Shipbuilders and that meant my national service would be deferred for five years while I finished training. I worked in the engine shop and was also on board the new *Ark Royal* during her sea trials in the Firth of Clyde—that trip was extended to seven days because of a gale.
>
> My plan was to serve my apprenticeship, then go to sea in the Merchant Navy. I often used to meet men who had done the same when they came back to the shipyard in between trips. They told me that unless I liked drinking beer, playing cards, and putting up with horrendous heat and humidity then the sea was no place to be. They were spinning a yarn, perhaps, but I also thought, hang on, there are no women at sea.
>
> So after three and a half years, I asked Cammell Lairds to let my deferment drop. I decided to get national service out of the way and in April 1955 I went into the RAF.

Reg Jones (RAF)

The general impression of national service is one of rigid and dogmatic regimes, where men were ordered from pillar to post with little or no room for individual judgement. That may have been the case on most occasions, but there were also times when individual requests and desires were taken into account:

> I was called up on 20 March 1947 and did my basic training at the Invicta Barracks in Maidstone with the Royal West Kents. I was then posted to the Royal Engineers Training Battalion. At the end of sapper training, I was selected for a cadre course, but I didn't want to spend two years training recruits in the UK. I wanted to go overseas and so they agreed and sent me the drafting depot at Barton Stacy.

Bryan Berry (Army)

Mistakes, altering postings, and changing your mind about beginning national service did not happen very often and for most of the new recruits it was not something they cared about anyway. For most of them, it was just a matter of waiting their time. The call up would come eventually, and once it did there was always an end in sight. There were several ways in which the young recruits got themselves through national service, including creating a demobilisation chart for their locker and logging off the days, and reading and re-reading letters from home. As Leslie Thomas's fictional hero in *The*

Virgin Soldiers comes to realise, the demobilisation chart and letters from a girlfriend were things that made life bearable:

> Strengthening smoke was rising from the wooden office buildings and someone was shouting. Brigg thought suddenly of all Joan's letters locked away in his desk over there. And his demobilisation chart.[12]

Demobilisation would come, but as men began their period of national service it seemed a long way off. For most new recruits, the eighteen months or two years of service in the armed forces seemed to stretch away interminably ahead of them, like a prison sentence they had neither wanted nor deserved.

Before then, there was also the comforting thought of offering those who came later the same advice that they, as new recruits, had been given by the veterans, already on their way back to Civvie Street. It was a phrase often thrown at them during their first few days in the service: 'get some in!'

2

Enlistment

By the terms of the National Service Act of 1948, all young men had to register for military service by the time they reached the qualifying age of eighteen. There was no escape from the registration process. Young men who did not register with the Ministry of Labour were quickly tracked down through public records, National Insurance, and so on, with fines, even imprisonment in some cases, resulting from a failure to add your name to the list.

There were several loopholes for exemptions or ways to delay the call up. These included exemptions for men in holy orders and for people who had serious illnesses, and deferments for those finishing an apprenticeship or a university course. For men engaged in apprenticeships or studying at college, it was only a temporary respite; once the period of study was over, the mailed fist of the military would inevitably close around the individual concerned.

For the vast majority of eighteen year olds, a week or two after registration they would receive orders to report to a designated assessment centre, often a Ministry of Labour office or the town hall, for a medical and further assessment. For some, the call was a shock, to others it was a welcome relief:

In 1956, I was working as a scientific assistant at the government atomic energy plant in Harwell. I hated the job, it was so boring, but my boss came in one day and told me he'd got me exempted because of the nature of my job at Harwell. I was a bit upset, thinking I'd have to stick the job a bit longer. Six months later, they asked me if I wanted to continue with the exemption. I said, 'No thanks, I'm going in.' I had my medical—A1. The Navy was full so I chose the RAF, mainly because I liked the choice of trades on offer. In the Army I'd have been driving a truck.

George Best (RAF)

My mother had died six months before I was called up. My father had died when I was very young so, really, there were just my brothers and me. It wasn't a great situation. When the call up letter arrived, I knew I could have got deferment because I'd just begun an apprenticeship as a compositor. But I thought, 'Money, food provided, lodgings, can't be bad. I'll take it.' And into the RAF I went. My boss wasn't happy; particularly as the law said he had to keep my job, and the apprenticeship, open for when I returned.

Alun Williams (RAF)

For some reason I wasn't ready for it when the letter arrived telling me to report for my medical. Of course, I knew national service was a possibility, but I'd put it out of my mind while I was doing my apprenticeship as a carpenter/joiner. So it came as a shock, a total shock for me, particularly as I was married and had a child when I was called up in March 1958. My son was just eleven months old. I asked for a compassionate home posting because of my family—no chance, the Army had plans for me.

Len Skipper (Army)

I didn't want to do national service—like lots of lads my age. It wasn't as if there was a war on and you were called to defend the country. That would have been different. But when my time came I was in the middle of an apprenticeship, designing aircraft undercarriage for Doughty. I kept taking more and more courses, more and more exams—AMIMECCI and other qualifications. Eventually I just ran out of courses to take and in May 1957 I received my call-up papers.

Brian Chaplin (RAF)

The first stage of the call-up process was the medical examination. It was something every potential recruit had to endure, regardless of their status or readiness to enlist and serve.

Medical examinations usually lasted a few hours and were daunting in an age of prudishness—particularly when the order came to drop your trousers. Recruits were rated in one of four grades. Grade I meant the man was fit for active service; Grade II was given if the doctors felt the recruit was not quite at Grade I level, but was capable of development; Grade III was issued to men fit only for sedentary jobs; and Grade IV meant that the man was given exemption on medical grounds as never being suitable for military service of any kind.

The medicals were followed by interviews and intelligence and aptitude tests, invariably taken on the same day. Such tests were hardly gruelling, sometimes as many as 200 young men being seated in the same exam hall, but this was the place to shine if you wanted a choice of service:

I was called to the assessment centre at Pownall Street in Liverpool. There must have been a couple of hundred boys there and, when it came to filling in the questionnaire, some of them were in trouble. They were struggling with phrases like 'infectious diseases' so I helped them out. At the end of the questionnaire it asked what Service you would like. I said the Royal Navy, never thinking I'd get it. But for some reason I did.

Bob Jackson (Navy)

I was living in Derby when I received my call-up letter. I went along to the recruiting office, as I was supposed to, and the sergeant asked me what I wanted to do with my life. I said I wanted to learn to drive. He nodded and said, 'The Army's the best place for you.' It was as simple as that.

Derek Grattidge (Army: Horse Guards)

When I went for my medical, they asked me for my preference. I didn't really mind where I went but I had a mate who had worked with me in the butcher's shop, name of Willie Lyndsey. He was a bit older than me so he was already in. He said I should opt for the RAF—'Come and join us,' he said. So that's what I did. I opted for the RAF and the next thing I knew I was on my way to RAF Padgate for training.

I suppose you didn't think about it at the time but that medical was quite important. I went through no problem but one of my mates, examined on the same day, was turned down—for having flat feet.

Ian Norrie (RAF Regiment)

I was at grammar school, having passed what was then known as the 11-plus examination. But I got a bang on the chest playing rugby and a tubular abscess came up. I was off school, more or less in bed the whole time, for a year. I did my A Levels and left school in 1947. I knew the call-up letter was coming and, to be honest, I didn't mind. I needed to know that everything was all right after the abscess. So when the letter arrived, I went off to Gloucester for the medical and, because of my history, they gave me an X-Ray. It was all okay and I was in.

Michael Beddis (RAF)

Often—but not always—what someone had done or was in the process of doing in 'Civvie Street' influenced where a man was sent for his service. Sometimes, would-be recruits could be proactive. This was particularly the case with the Navy:

I was sent to the Royal Navy, probably because I was working for a Stevedore Company in Liverpool Docks at the time. So I knew all about derricks, blocks and tackle, ropes and knots, and so on. It probably helped. Mind you, I later served with several national service sailors and they had had absolutely no previous experience of ships and boats. So who knows?

Larry Burrell (Navy)

In 1956–57, I was working as a junior clerk for a firm of solicitors in Fleet Street in London. I knew national service was coming and someone had told me it would help me get the service I wanted if I could show I had previous experience. So I joined the Royal Naval Volunteer Reserve. I was just sixteen years old and we used to train on an old ship—HMS *President*, I think—that was moored on the Thames. For a full year I did that, training in the evenings and at weekends in communication and radio.

Noel Smith (Navy)

I was called up in 1955. I had just finished my apprenticeship as a joiner and when they looked at my details and asked what I'd like to do I said I'd like to follow my trade. Well, I'd spent several years learning it. They said we always need men to build and repair roads; that type of thing. The Royal Engineers seemed appropriate and that's where I went.

Brian Wheeler (Army)

I had joined the RNVR in 1955 in the hope that it would guarantee me a place in the Navy when my time came. It worked for me so those evenings and weekends spent at HMS *Cambria* and on a sea going coastal minesweeper were worth it. But one friend of mine, a stoker from the RNVR, didn't get in. When he went for his medical it turned out he was colour blind. There was always that element of pot luck.

Terry Colburn (Navy)

Many new recruits were pragmatic about where they went, just accepting what fate had in store for them. Others were far more determined to get exactly what they wanted; after all, it was two years out of your life and they were going to work hard to get the best posting they could. For some, their fate remained an absolute mystery until the call-up papers dropped through the letterbox:

After I left school I worked on the railway. I didn't get called up until I was well past eighteen. My birthday was in the summer, but no call came until I was about eighteen and a half. I reckon it was all to do with helping British Rail cope with the summer rush. That was how most people went on holiday in those days, on the train.

But in October 1952 I got my letter. I ended up in the Army Catering Corps. God knows why. The only thing I can think of is that, at my medical, I happened to mention that I'd done the cooking when my mum was taken ill.

Alec Maxwell (Army)

I was called up on 1 May 1951. It was own fault, really. I was articled to an accountant and had already been deferred for two years. I could have carried on like that, but national service was always there, in the background, waiting. I wasn't very happy in work and decided to push my luck. I asked the boss for a raise. 'How much?' he asked.

'Ten shillings a week extra,' I said. He went ballistic and told me there was no way I was going to get that. So I quit, knowing that the call up was now inevitable. Within a few weeks, I'd been called to Gloucester for my medical and then off to Devizes for basic training and life in the Army Pay Corps.

Gordon Denley (Army)

I was born in London, Kensal Rise, but was evacuated to Wales during the war. I even learned to speak Welsh. After the war, I was working on the railway, running fast freight to Swindon and beyond. When the call-up letter came I didn't mind. I was young and fit, a games player, and I wanted to see a bit of the world. So, in a way, I was looking forward to it. This was 1955 and I was just eighteen years old.

I went for my medical in Cardiff with a mate. We didn't fancy the coarse Army shirts so he said, 'Let's go for the RAF.' I agreed, but I didn't want an office job. I wanted to be out in the open air. They said I could have the RAF Regiment—the Rock Apes as they called us—but I'd have to sign on for an extra year. Two years, three years, it didn't bother me. And you got a bit of extra pay for the third year. So that's what I did.

John Williams (RAF Regiment)

Sometimes it paid to be a little dogmatic. It did not guarantee a preferred placement or service, but it did at least show the men in charge that you cared about where you ended up:

At my selection interview, the petty officer said I could be a seaman, a stoker, or a cook. I told him I wanted to be a coder. The PO didn't know anything about coders except that you'd have to go to London for selection. Off I went, my dad with me, and I was met by a Wren officer who was very apologetic. The commander, she explained, had been called away. I said to my father to go off and have a look around but to come back and check on me every hour, just in case.

The Wren officer and I went to the top floor of this office block. She said, 'I know nothing about coders except there are one on every ship and two on every aircraft carrier.'

We talked for a while then she beckoned me over to the window and, knowing I had never been to London before, she pointed out all the sights. 'Go and see them before you leave,' she said. I was back down, out the front, waiting for my dad in ten minutes. And that was it. I was accepted as a coder.

Bob Jackson (Navy)

Bob Jackson had done his homework. He had already been told that, in the post-war period, at the height of the Cold War, the Royal Navy had two types of coder. He knew that he would have to make a decision about which one he would prefer. The first type was taught Russian—at the Navy's expense—then posted to a trawler somewhere in the North Sea. His job was to listen to Russian radio transmissions and broadcasts, then transmit them back to the UK where the vital (or not so vital) information would be disseminated:

> I didn't fancy sitting up there in the North Sea or off the coast of Scandinavia—too cold by half. So I opted for the second type. This was an educational coder and the purpose was to help young seamen, to educate them. I'd never done any type of teaching before, but I was willing to give it a chance and, looking back now, I'm glad I did.
>
> Bob Jackson (Navy)

Once the medical and initial assessments were completed, the new recruits would be sent home to await the formal summons to come and serve. The length of wait varied, but it was generally in the region of six to eight weeks. It was not long to tidy up affairs, say goodbye to girlfriends (or wives), and get your hair cut in the hope of escaping the tender mercies of the unit barber.

Soon—too soon for some, too late for others—the summons came. For some reason, Thursday was the day for the departure of new recruits, 6,000 of them each fortnight, from their homes. They were all headed for training bases across the country. It was a seething mass of humanity, hundreds of nervous youths all trying to act confident— and all fooling absolutely nobody:

> All over England that morning trains had drawn out of stations, out of great termini, and out of village halts, their carriages full of callow youths in varying mood of confidence, apprehension and fear.[1]

Strangely for some, the call never came, as Derick Northrop can testify:

> I had my medical, was told that I was going into the Navy and sent home to wait. I waited and waited, but no call up came. I was engaged to be married and needed to know what was going on so I went to the recruiting office in Bradford. I told the sergeant-major about my problem. He asked my date of birth and I told him, 12 December 1928. He said, 'Go home and don't worry about it. Nobody in the two-week period around your birthday ever gets called.' He was right—I never did receive the call up.
>
> Derick Northrop

Quite why Derick Northrop was never called to serve in the Navy has never been made clear. He has asked many times, but has never been given a logical or satisfactory answer. A few years later, he did meet a man, Eddie Baron from Halifax, whose birthday was within a few days of his own. He, too, had had the same experience, also without any form of explanation. Derick Northrop's case was rare. For the 2.5 million young men who entered the armed forces as national service conscripts between 1945 and 1963, there was no such luck.

For some, entering into service with the armed forces was nothing new. Brinley Robbin had actually enlisted as a boy apprentice in the RAF when he was just sixteen years of age. He was out again within eight months:

> I was the baby of the family and my mother insisted I come out as all the other children had left home. I argued with my mother but as I was under the legal age to make decisions like that, her word was law. So out I came. I started an apprenticeship with a garage and so national service was deferred until I was twenty-one years of age. I could have gone back into the RAF, but I had friends who had gone into the RAF and spent their whole time sitting in a field in Hampshire. I thought the Army might offer me a bit more adventure.

> Brinley Robbin (Army)

Whether the would-be servicemen waited in trepidation or expectation, the call up soon came, the letters dropping with a clash of thunder onto the doormats of houses all over the country. For some, it meant total disruption of their plans:

> I received my call-up papers on a Thursday in June 1956. The only trouble was I was getting married on the Saturday. I wrote, explaining the situation and got a letter back saying, 'Congratulation. You can come in with the next intake in a fortnight.' Wonderful, I thought.

> Brian Collins (Army)

The new recruits were given rail warrants or postal orders for the fare and this meant that they invariably travelled to their first camp together:

> I served from September 1947 until October 1949 and never left Britain. I remember getting on the train, leaving the station, lots of us all heading for RAF Padgate. We didn't stay there long, it was just a place to register and get kitted out. Within a few days we were all off to West Kirby for the routine stretch of 'square bashing'. But that train to Padgate was where we met lots of new friends. There were all sorts. One chap, a dentist in civilian life, he didn't know his arse from his elbow. As we found out, just trying to keep his equipment clean was a major problem. He couldn't dress himself properly in his uniform and we had to help him. His kit was always in a terrible state. If we hadn't been helping him out goodness knows what would have happened to him.

> Brian Swain (RAF)

I can still remember my first morning in the RAF. They lined us up on the square, the parade ground, and the NCOs starting bellowing orders for anybody who'd played rugby, football, whatever, for their county or country to come forward. That was one thing about the forces, you were guaranteed a good time of it if you played sport to a reasonable level. Alan Priday, the rugby player, was in the same intake as me and when it came to his first posting, where did he get? St Athan because he played for Cardiff which was just 15 miles away from the RAF station.

Alun Williams (RAF)

On arrival at their base, the new recruits were usually met at a central railway station by a military truck and an NCO or petty officer. Immediately, they began to learn a whole new language that went with their new way of life. Words like 'blanco', 'spit and polish', 'Bull'—'Bullshit' to give it the full name—'jankers', and so on.[2]

Men from all walks of life were suddenly thrown together and it was not just life styles that were different. For the first time, men from cities like London encountered Scottish or northern accents:

There were about eighty lads in out intake, lots of Englishmen, particularly Londoners, and guys from the Midlands, about five Scots, and a few Welshmen. They were from all walks of life, mostly about eighteen years old. The older fellows were twenty-three to twenty-five and were qualified accountants and lawyers and engineers. We even had one really slow-spoken chap from the Fens; he told us he was a poacher. We kidded him about his speech, to which ribbing he eventually responded, 'Oi doant tawwwk broad—it's just the way Oi speeek.'

Colin MacCallum (RAF)

It was not just speech patterns or accents that were different. Men were thrown together, regardless of social class or upbringing, and very often that meant socialising and living with people they would otherwise never have met and certainly never have spoken to:

The fellow on my immediate right sobbed piteously during the night, calling for his mother. At the far end, nearest the door, was a bullet-headed, cauliflower-eared young tough from Glasgow, monosyllabic, emanating a general malevolence. Honing my embryonic social skills, I took my boots and 'bulling' polish and sat with him, asking for his story. He was in for nine years, having been ordered by a court in Glasgow to join the Army, if they would take him, or to take some sort of civil punishment. He had killed a member of a rival teen gang in Glasgow, knocking him over a balcony and breaking his neck. It was a rich mix of characters all right.

Bev Steele (Army)

Perhaps for the first time, the new recruits, most of them still young and relatively protected, encountered prejudice, even racism. For young lads, often away from home for the first time in their lives, such attitudes were difficult to fathom:

> In our hut at Aldershot, we had a wide range of boys, Geordies, Scots, and Cockneys—very difficult to understand. I'd never seen or heard anything like it. The corporal in charge came storming in, bellowing in his Cockney voice, 'First of all, any Welshmen here. Hold up your hands.' Me and a few others did. Then he snarled. 'I'll let you know now, I hate the Welsh. You're in for a real hard time.' And we were. He gave us every dirty job he could think of—and I still don't know why.

> Ron Evans (Army)

Such bigotry did not have to have any reason or rationale; it was just something with which the young men had to deal. Dealing with it was what they did, and it was a quick learning curve for most of the new recruits:

> The NCOs were absolute dictators. Their word was all that mattered. You'd fold your kit to what you thought was perfection and they'd come along and tip it all up—just for the fun of it. But eventually you learned. You knew when to say, 'Yes, sir, No sir, three bags full sir.' But it was a case of learn or find yourself in real trouble.

> Gordon Denley (Army)

> Basic training? You hear lots of stories about the brutality and so on. Yes, it was tough, but we were young and lots of us were used to harshness. I'd been educated at a Jesuit College—now that was tough. You could say it prepared me for the Navy.

> Larry Burrell (Navy)

If the recruits had begun to learn, so too did officialdom, albeit from a different end of the spectrum. That first camp, before basic training had even begun, was where the Army, Navy, or RAF really started to find out about their new recruits:

> You had to give your religion. I was never particularly religious but I told them [I was] Welsh Methodist. 'Stop pissing about,' said the petty officer. 'I've never heard of it and I can't spell it anyway. So as of now you're C of E.'

> Geoff Lewis (Navy)

The word 'new' was central to everything—a new way of life, new friends and enemies, and new experiences. The whole world was suddenly new.

3

Basic Training

Basic training, whatever service you joined, was central to the myth of national service brutality. It was when beds were turned upside down or flung across the floor, when carefully folded kit was hurled through open windows onto wet tarmac, and men were made to weed flower beds with knives and forks. At least, that was the legend, possibly with some elements of truth: 'When the legend grows bigger than the truth, print the legend.'

What is certain about basic training is that the parade ground was where young, raw recruits were 'broken in'.[1] The whole purpose behind the hated, seemingly mindless drilling that new recruits endured was to develop an instinctive sense of obedience so that in crisis and battle situations discipline would hold firm, whatever chaos was going on around them. The national servicemen reacted to the pressures and problems of basic training according to their personalities or character:

> I did my 'square bashing' at Padgate. It lasted for just over eight weeks. That was because I was bound for the RAF Regiment. Normally, basic training was shorter for the RAF boys. It was all bullshit, of course, but I was fit and young and took it in my stride. I tell you, though, it was nothing to what I was to get later on with the Rock Apes.
>
> John Williams (RAF Regiment)

> I enjoyed basic training, even got 'Best Recruit'. I also won a medal for gymnastics. Of course you got your kit thrown around by the NCOs, which was par for the course. There was nothing personal in it. It was just something that they did. No, I loved it all. If I hadn't been married I think I'd have signed on as a regular.
>
> Brian Wheeler (Army)

> I found basic training soul destroying. It was all so pointless; you had to do really stupid things. It was all based around square bashing, of course, with sergeants and

corporals screaming and shouting abuse. And then I got German measles. They sent me off to the RAF Hospital at Cosford and that was really boring, nothing to do but sit in bed all day. To make matters worse when I got out of hospital I was re-flighted—I had to go back to finish off basic training.

George Best (RAF)

Basic training was moronic. We were in Nissen huts, beds each side and one central stove to heat the whole place. In came the corporal—'By the morning I want this floor shining like a new shilling in a black sheep's arsehole.' A right comedian.

We worked half the night and we still had to be up by 6.30 a.m., then wash in cold water and dress in blue serge. Corporal arrives again and we all stand to attention. He saw a little piece of fluff on the floor and went ape. 'This place is a fucking disgrace; I nearly broke my neck on this great pile of shit!' Of course we all fell about laughing. He tore up all the beds and put the whole hut on a charge.

The best laugh we ever had was when he came prancing in and picked on one of the lads—'Smith, you're standing there like a pregnant duck. What have you got to say for yourself?' The response was obvious—'Quack, quack!' All of us on a charge again.

Brian Chaplin (RAF)

I felt okay about the call up and basic training. I'd been in the cadet force in school at Brecon, so I was used to wearing uniform and, as it had been a boarding school, it meant nothing to me to be living in a barracks room. I took it in my stride—in fact, I used to press the other lads uniforms for them. At a shilling a time it was a good little earner, considering how poorly we were paid.

David Lloyd (Army)

Strange as it may seem, I actually enjoyed basic training. Yes, there was lots of shouting, but I can't remember many swear words or personal abuse, nobody screaming to get your hair cut or anything like that. It was just the sight of 100 or more blokes, all marching in step, in perfect unison. It was almost balletic in my opinion.

Reg Gooding (RAF)

We did our basic training on the Yorkshire Moors. It was the winter of 1955 and there was snow on the ground. I still don't know how it related to service in the Navy, but temperatures were sub-zero. The petty officers were brutal and gave us a hard time. Most of them had served in the Second World War and I think they were taking it out on us.

Trevor Pickering (Navy)

Square bashing was the worst, most depressing part of my life. To be at RAF Hednesford in Cannock Chase, in what had been a POW Camp during the First World War, without heat in May, with the snow coming down and the prospect of all those idiot drill instructors screaming at all these helpless eighteen year olds, I just couldn't understand it.

Reg Jones (RAF)

The corporal or petty officer's word was law. All of the NCOs expected instant obedience, just like they expected the recruits to laugh at their jokes. Recruits soon learned that they crossed these tyrants at their peril.

I can't say that the NCOs frightened me, although they certainly had that effect on some of the lads. No, I was over twenty and I'd spent three years in a shipyard so I was used to shouting and being pushed around. I didn't see the point of it all, I must say, but fear? No. Mind you they certainly did have power and control and you learned, pretty quickly, to do whatever they wanted.

Reg Jones (RAF)

The length of basic training varied from service to service. The Navy, which only took around 3,000 new recruits each year, tended to keep men in basic training for about four weeks, after which they were sent off for specialised instruction according to the work they would have to do. In the early days of national service, before centralised posting was introduced, men were allocated to one of the Navy's traditional three shore bases—Plymouth, Portsmouth, or Chatham—but they were only the nominal draft centres or divisions, the actual training could take place almost anywhere. The RAF tended to limit its 'square bashing' to just six weeks, although for men of the RAF Regiment, which had many ceremonial duties as well as its policing work, it could and usually did last longer. The Army ran its basic training programmes for considerably longer, sometimes for as much as three months at a time.

After his initiation at RAF Cardington, Colin MacCallum had hopes of being sent to Wilmslow. There were, apparently, 3,000 WAAFs stationed there. Instead, on 14 May 1954, he and his mates found themselves posted to Hednesford in Staffordshire to complete their basic training:

We were all up before six o'clock and, having spruced up the billet and handed in our linen, we were all on the square with full kit by nine o'clock. The buses were already there, eleven of them, but through one thing and another we stood on the square, more or less at attention, until after eleven o'clock.

Colin MacCallum (RAF)

Whether the delay was bureaucracy at work or just the bloody mindedness of the NCOs was never clear, but, at last, the recruits left:

> The buses were pretty comfortable and cosy and we got to the camp just before two o'clock. We were all sitting in a bit of a daze, looking out of the windows at a desolate piece of land; nothing but pine forest, all a sinister dark green, almost black, and a cold, wet mist swirling everywhere, down into the gullies and across the boulder-strewn clearings. There wasn't a house in sight—just rows and rows of long, low, unwelcoming, dark brown huts. The door of the bus suddenly opened and an immaculate corporal leapt in, screaming, 'Get out of the f-g buses,' and we hurtled out the door onto the long wet grass. Then the corporal was screaming, "Get off the f-g grass,' so we did, in total confusion. Then it was, 'Get into that f-g hut.' Hut 109, our home for the next two months.

Colin MacCallum (RAF)

Occasionally, for reasons that were often beyond the understanding of the new conscripts, basic training was extended or cut short, seemingly on a mere whim, as Ken Williams found out. It was perhaps inevitable that when his basic training was reduced in length it was not a gift from the Army, but it was at the expense of his evenings and weekends:

> I joined the Army in 1949, one of the first batch of post-war national servicemen. I did my basic training at Blandford and when I arrived we were told by our NCO that we'd be training night and day. That's what we did, bulling and marching by day, listening to lectures and more bulling of equipment each night. It was exhausting, but it did cut short the basic training period. It turned out that the colonel was retiring and they wanted a spectacular passing-out parade for him, hence the rush to get us trained.

Ken Williams (Army)

For many new recruits, one of the first experiences of basic training was the haircut. Aimed at making everyone look the same and, maybe, to stop head lice, it was almost a ceremonial occasion where 'the loss of the carefully grown, coiffed and Brylcreemed Teddy Boy DA haircut was a tragedy to some'.[2]

A tragedy for some, but cleverly avoided by others:

> I did my basic training in Worcester and it was hard. They didn't mess about those boys. The first day, we were marched up to the barber. I watched him—it was as if he was cutting hedges, clippers up the back of the neck and over the top of your skull. Now I'd been badly burned when I was a nipper and I had a scar on the back of my neck. I explained and showed the barber—'You cut that,' I said, 'and it won't stop bleeding.'

He took one look and said, 'Get out of the chair. I'm not going anywhere near that.' That was it—I was excused haircuts for the rest of my national service. I got a 'chitty' from the MO and whenever anyone screamed at me to get my hair cut I just flashed the piece of paper at them.

Brian Collins (Army)

Basic training was not just about running around the Barrack Square or refolding kit when irate drill instructors had hurled it onto the floor—although there were plenty of both for all recruits. It was also when the new soldiers learned the necessary skills of housekeeping—things that had probably been done by their mothers before the call up:

Basic training was when I learned to use a needle and thread. Sewing buttons onto tunics and darning holes was all part of the process. We had several 'toffs' in our section and they had no idea—they probably had servants to sew and darn for them in civilian life. Our darning was pretty bad but at least it covered the holes. Theirs was just awful.

Ian Norrie (RAF Regiment)

Food was fairly basic, but it was plentiful. The recruits, many of them engaged in more physical activity than they had ever dreamed possible before enlistment, needed carbohydrates and food that would give them energy. The standard cartoon or image of a soldier on jankers sitting before a mound of waiting potatoes was not far from the truth:

Everybody has heard the term spud bashing—that's what they called it. We all had a turn of it sooner or later, mountains of potatoes that had to be peeled. Normally you'd use your Army 'jack knife', but I managed to get hold of five potato peelers. I hired them out to whoever was on spud bashing that particular day.

David Lloyd (Army)

For my basic training I was at Aldershot. I must have been there for about two months. The food was filling, but the way it was served left a lot to be desired. You'd go up with your tray and they'd just slap it on. Often your dinner and your afters were all mixed together. To start with you'd try to separate them but after a while you just ate it all together. You were so hungry you'd eat anything. Later, when I went to Germany, the food was the best I ever tasted in the Army and they even had waiter and waitress service. But Aldershot? It was terrible.

Ron Evans (Army)

For many of the new recruits, it seemed as if they were destined to spend their life polishing boots, belt buckles, webbing, and even the billet floor, which had to be constantly massaged with a bumper, cloth, and wax until it shone. Trying to polish the dimples out of the coarse ammunition boots that were issued to all new soldiers was a real problem:

> All our boots—rock-hard, unbendable leather—had these dimples across the toe caps and the heels. The only way to get rid of them was to polish them out. You'd layer on polish, then heat it up and massage the stuff with the back of an old toothbrush. Some boys used the back of their spoon but whatever instrument you used it was polish, polish, polish. And, eventually, the dimples began to disappear.
>
> Henry Jones (Army)

> The boots were all hard leather, covered in these tiny pimples that you had to get rid of. I've seen guys iron them or, usually, smooth them out with the back of a hot spoon. On parade you'd get the drill sergeants or corporals poking at them with their swagger sticks—'These boots are manky!' they'd scream. And it brought tears to your eyes because you'd spent hours polishing and smoothing and rubbing the things.
>
> John Gibson (Army)

> Getting the uniforms right was a nightmare. Polishing boots with your thumb inside a spoon and rubbing round and round in little circles; ironing creases into your trousers; it seemed to go on forever. We might not have been able to fight, but we could certainly polish. We had little weights at the bottom of our trousers so that they'd hang down over the puttees just right. The beret was a real hit or miss affair. Some blokes just couldn't get it right—badge in the middle of your forehead, hold it tight to your head and then twist the beret into shape. After a few weeks it took on its proper shape—if you were lucky.
>
> Ian Norrie (RAF Regiment)

Then, of course, there were injections:

> After lunch we were all given a yellow disc to mount behind our cap badges to distinguish our intake from the others. Then we had vaccinations for smallpox and blood tests. That evening, although it had been a long and quite stressful day, we had lectures all evening in one of the huts. During the lectures ever so many of the chaps fainted and were carted outside and laid on the grass to recover. After about the fourth such fainting, the corporal yelled at us that it was 'mass hysteria,

that's all', and another four fellows fainted in the next hour and were duly lugged outside. It transpired that most of those men who had fainted had also had a tetanus injection.

Colin MacCallum (RAF)

We had to line up for the regulation series of injections. It was just one needle—they filled up the syringe each time but the needle was the same. I suppose there was sterilisation of some sort, hygiene to a point, but all those blokes were being injected with the same needle. It doesn't bear thinking about. It was okay if you were dealt with first but the thing pretty soon became blunt. I guess that's why lots of men fainted.

Ian Norrie (RAF Regiment)

Those injections—we all had to endure them but some managed better than others. I remember standing in line with all the rest and in front of me was this big, 6-foot bloke. He was sweating. And then he just keeled over, out like a light. That was before they even stuck the needle in his arm.

David Lloyd (Army)

Little allowance was given for illness or homesickness. The cushy life in Civvie Street was over, they were in the forces now and they would have to adjust:

I remember lying in my bed at night listening to some of the other boys crying. I felt sorry for them, but, I suppose, it depended on your home life. My upbringing had been hard, so I don't say I was used to it, but I didn't feel the homesickness like some. I was at Padgate in March and it was bitterly cold. Even so, they used to put us in PE kit for cross country runs—it'll toughen you up, the NCOs said. I can still remember the girls we passed shouting after us and cat calling.

We used to look at the boys who'd been there a few weeks. They all looked so much older than us—and so professional. They'd survived the corporals and the drill sergeants who were there to break you. No doubt about that, it was their job. Our corporal, he didn't make friends with any of us. That wasn't his job. Every night he'd open the door of his room and throw his webbing, gaiters, etc. onto the floor. He didn't say a word, but we had to clean them. One night we rebelled, left them there. My God, did he make our lives hell. After that we dived on his gear whenever it appeared— lesson learned.

For fatigues, we had to wash and clean the wash buildings and the toilets. We used two hose pipes and a couple of squeegees. My boots were soaking and I tried to dry them by putting them on the stove all night. The next morning the toe caps had turned up, facing the sky. They split right across the soles and I had to apply for a new pair.

Alun Williams (RAF)

Basic training was only the start of life in the forces. It was like an initiation, something everyone had to endure and get through as painlessly as possible. It was not the real Army or Navy or RAF, something everyone had to try to remember.

As basic training neared its end, the recruits were faced with aptitude tests and interviews to determine what trade they would follow for the next two years. It was an important moment, but for some the choices came even earlier in their basic training:

I was with the 17th/21st Lancers, a Tank Regiment in those days, at Catterick and after about ten days they gave us aptitude tests to determine where we were to go, what we were to do. I remember thinking it was a bit early, but you didn't complain or question, you just did what you were told.

I was called in to see the Personnel Selection Officer and he told me that the regiment had to send so many men each year to the Household Cavalry at Windsor and that I'd been chosen to be one of them.

I'd heard about the bull and all the pomp and ceremony down there with the Household Cavalry so I said I'd rather stay where I was, thank you very much. He grinned at me, 'Tough luck,' he said. 'You're going—tomorrow.'

Derek Grattidge (Army)

Complaining was never an option, you simply had to follow orders and go where you were sent. It was much easier for everyone if you just accepted your lot:

I did my basic training in Aldershot, Gibraltar Barracks. They'd been built in the Boer War and they were miserable, cold, and wet. I didn't mind too much because I was young and fit and, by and large, I kept my nose clean. But living conditions could have been a lot better. Basic training was all bull and marching, but then, about half way through, they offered me a B4 Driving Course, learning to drive heavy vehicles. It meant time off basic training and away from Gibraltar Barracks so I took it. That was in October 1951 and after finishing the course I went straight into the Royal Engineers.

Brinley Robbin (Army)

At the end of basic training I went before the board to decide on a trade. There was a long list to choose from but I chose only the one—navigator. To get that, they told me, I'd have to sign on for three years. 'Sod that,' I said and chose radar operator instead.

'I'm either going to be one of those,' I said, 'or you can do what you like with me.' And amazingly I got it, a radar operator I became.

George Best (RAF)

When we had our tests to determine which trade we would follow I opted for air wireless. It was approved and I went off for three months training at Yatesbury. And then they decided that people doing national service would not train in mechanics as it was just not worth it. So I was trained as an air wireless assistant instead.

Michael Beddis (RAF)

For those who wanted to take the opportunity, there was also the possibility of a commission. The Army and the RAF earmarked likely candidates at an early stage of their training, nominating such men as potential officers, but still insisting that they complete their basic training with the rest of their squad. For Brian Chaplin, who had already considered trying for a commission before he was called up for national service, the offer was too good a chance to miss—even though it brought with it more than a little unpleasantness and trouble:

The NCOs came around asking if anyone would like to become an officer. Why not, I thought, and stuck my hand up. I only had a few weeks of basic training to do, but they made my life a misery for the rest of that time. Picked on? You could say. 'You'll never make an officer as long as you've got a hole in your arse,' they'd say. I was really glad to finish basic training and get away for the War Office Selection Board.

Brian Chaplin (RAF)

Doctors and dentists had not been included in the list of exempted professions, but they did at least know that once their professional training was complete they would be granted a commission in whichever service they chose.

The poet and writer Dannie Abse was called up into the RAF in May 1951 and, although he was sent for what he called 'modified square bashing' at Moreton-in-the-Marsh, he knew that as an officer and a doctor he was privileged. He would not have to endure the induction to the RAF that the 'erks' would all face. A gentle, self-effacing man, Dannie Abse always felt himself to be something of an imposter in the RAF. Fellow officers called him 'Doc' and he could never get used to being saluted. Despite the privilege of officer and doctor status, Abse's commanding officer left him in no doubt where his priorities lay—'Don't forget,' he barked, 'you must consider yourself an RAF officer first and a doctor second.'[3]

Bryan Griffiths graduated in medicine at Charring Cross Hospital and went into the Army in February 1958. He had asked for the Navy, but to get that he would have had to take a Short Service Commission, which lasted for three years:

Two years was enough for me and so I went in to the Army. Basic training for me lasted just six weeks. The first two were standard basic training, learning how to march, salute, and grasp some rudiments of military etiquette. Then there were another two weeks at the Royal Army Medical College and these put the emphasis on things like tropical medicine and management of battle casualties. The final two weeks were at Mytchett Camp, close to Aldershot, and dealt with Army health, making sure camps had good drainage, things like that.

Bryan Griffiths (Army: Royal Army Medical Corps)

For some men, basic training was cut short by factors they could not control. It may have jolted them out of newly established routines, but they were not going to argue; after all, not that many of them wanted to go back for a longer stint of square bashing:

I was doing my basic training at Ranby Camp. It was supposed to last ten weeks, but after six, for some reason, they let us home on leave. It was an unexpected treat— in more ways than one. While I was at home on leave I caught tonsillitis. I guess it was some sort of reaction to the conditions I'd been enduring but it meant I had to stay in Cheltenham for the next six weeks. As I was already a qualified mechanic they said don't bother with the rest of basic training. They sent me on a driving course in Chester instead.

Arthur Ainger (Army)

I was already a member of the RNVR when I was called up in November 1957. I went for my basic training at HMS *Victory*—the barracks in Portsmouth, not on board Nelson's old ship—but for the first four weeks of training we weren't allowed 'ashore'. That was fairly standard and applied to all new recruits.

The food in the barracks was abysmal, partly because it was so badly prepared, so badly cooked, and partly because we had just joined up and were away from mum's cooking for the first time. You had to eat it, there was nothing else, but I can't say I enjoyed any of it. You just sat there and stuffed it in.

But after four weeks they let us ashore. First stop, the NAAFI in Portsmouth. I don't think I've ever eaten such an enormous meal or such a tasty one.

Terry Colburn (Navy)

Sometimes finding the right option was difficult and many men were forced to take their second or even third choice of trade. Sometimes there was no choice at all:

I tried out for aircrew and they found that I was astigmatic and had a perforated ear drum. So that option was quickly dispensed with.

Then they asked if I'd like to try for a commission. It would mean signing on for three years but three years—despite the fact that I'd been in the Combined Cadet Force at school and was senior cadet at the Hednesford Potential Officer Material Camp—sounded a bit long for me.

I suggested that with my engineering and marine background maybe air-sea rescue would be a good idea. 'Sign up for thirteen years,' they said, 'and you can have air-sea rescue.' I was amazed, but apparently there was no shortage of volunteers in that particular branch of the service.

In the end I became a radar operator. I chose it because the length of time doing 'trade training' was the shortest and, at that stage, I didn't think there would be that much difference between square bashing and trade training. That wasn't strictly true, but I only discovered that later.

They posted me to RAF Langtoft near Market Deeping and made me an acting corporal. And then the Suez Crisis blew up.

Reg Jones (RAF)

I did my basic training at HMS *Raleigh*, Torpoint. I had recently finished my apprenticeship as a joiner so I was twenty-one when I went in. I remember saying to the officer, 'Look here, mate, I'm not going to be a stoker. If that's all you've got I'll go to the Army instead.' And that's why I finished up being—you've guessed it—a stoker.

Patrick Line (Navy)

All recruits had been promised that, sooner or later, they would be treated to the 'delights' of the gas chamber. It was something that the NCOs hinted at with more than a degree of relish and most recruits shivered when they even thought about it—the connotations with the recent disclosures about Hitler's death camps were too close for comfort and it was not something they looked forward to:

We fitted our respirators and then marched into the hut. A corporal from the RAF Regiment lit a couple of little capsules on a saucer in the middle of the floor and then walked us around the hut at a slow double, still with our masks on.

After a couple of minutes he told us to think of a song, then to take off our masks and, finally, to sing it; all this to stop us holding our breath. It took no time at all for the gas to have us all with burning noses, mouths and throats, running eyes, and choking while we staggered around, feebly trying to sing that ruddy song 'On Ilkley Moor Baht 'at' in between choking gasps for air.

We were then ordered outside and told to race for the NAAFI—by the time we'd run there we'd pretty well recovered.

Colin MacCallum (RAF)

We'd all heard about the gas chamber, the corporals seemed to take a delight in telling us what was coming. Our time finally arrived and in we went—without masks. We coughed and spluttered for a few minutes, then were allowed out. I still think it was a total waste of time, just more chances for the NCOs to show you who was boss, but all the gas in that room certainly brought tears to your eyes.

Ian Norrie (RAF Regiment)

The final weeks of basic training were hectic. For the first time, the men got to fire real weapons as opposed to just polishing them. For lots of the new recruits, firing guns was a totally new experience, something they approached with awe and trepidation. Nevertheless, it was something they all had to do, regardless of their trade. Instruction was, in the main, gentler than on the barrack square, but even so many of the recruits were soon sporting bruised shoulders from the recoil of rifle and Bren guns:

The Bren gun was a lovely piece of machinery. It wasn't water cooled and was just like a short machine gun with two legs under the barrel. It was a lovely gun that just fired strips of bullets. The .22 rifle was another good weapon. It was like a sniper rifle and was used by infantry in jungle warfare, much lighter than the old .303.

But the Sten gun was no good at all. It was cheap and nasty and would always be failing, jamming every other burst. I think it was a Second World War design, a good ten years out of date. We hated it.

John Gibson (Army)

I was detailed to join HMS *Cumberland* but between finishing my course and joining, I went for a series of small arms and assault training courses at a base over the river, close to Raleigh. We did assault courses and things like that and fired Lanchesters, which were the naval equivalent of the Sten gun.

Then I heard they were looking for a replacement for the Devonport Field Gun Crew. I put my name forward and forgot about it. One day, going back to barracks, one of the instructors came in—'Which of you bastards is Colburn?' he shouted. I wondered what I'd done wrong, but it was the field gun application.

They gave me a test, which consisted of picking up a gun carriage wheel, running with it, and throwing it over a wall. Then they told me I was in. I went back to barracks at HMS *Cambridge* and waited. The call came and I was all packed up, my gear in the back of the lorry when they came with instructions from central drafting—a new thing then as, previously, you were either a Devonport, Chatham, or Portsmouth man.

It seemed that you couldn't join the field gun crew until you had some sea time in. And, of course, I hadn't. So it was back to my original draft on HMS *Cumberland*.

Terry Colburn

After the delights of the firing range and the rifle butts, there was the dubious 'pleasure' of the assault course. Every training camp had one and every recruit had to endure its rigours:

> We started in details of four at two-minute intervals. We, the second detail, got off to a good start over a ditch filled with barbed wire, up a hill to the second obstacle— barbed wire stretched between posts about a foot from the ground. A thunder flash exploded right in front of me and the other Scotsman in the detail yelled, 'I bet that's blown Colin's heid aff!' It hadn't.

Colin MacCallum

After several more obstacles, tunnels, and bridges—all the while with thunder flashes and blanks exploding all around them—Colin MacCallum's detail came to the rope swing:

> I overtook a couple of fellows from the first detail, then jumped about 9 feet from the end of the bridge to the ground and ran up to the rope swing over the water pit where there was a flying officer and a corporal with fire hoses, spraying everyone who came along.
>
> The corporal swinging the rope swung it too soon—on purpose I guess—and I caught it too low down and fell off into the water.
>
> I scrambled out as quickly as my water-logged denims and boots would allow, up and over the hair net, rolled over a 6-foot high wall in classic fashion, then some wretch of a corporal from the RAF Regiment flung a thunder flash on the bridge and I got a big bruise on my shoulder to show for it.

Colin MacCallum

After that, it was simply a case of rehearsals for the passing out parade and waiting for the moment they could leave camp. When their basic training came to an end, the national servicemen were no longer recruits. They were now soldiers, sailors, or airmen, men who were ready to move onto the next stage in their training and service life.

4

Trade Training

In post-war Britain, resources were scarce and none of the three services were ever going to spend vast amounts of time, money, and effort on training men who, at best, had only eighteen months to pay back any investment the military might make. Nevertheless, trade training of some sort was still required after the formal passing out parade and, if they were lucky, in the wake of an all-too-brief spot of leave:

One of the older lads—a fully qualified accountant from Glasgow—told us that we wouldn't have much fun on leave because they put bromide in our tea to curb our sexual instincts. That caused significant consternation. Like most of the fellows, I stopped drinking tea about five days before the leave began.

Colin MacCallum (RAF)

Following Christmas leave, it was by train to the main training camp on the Welsh coast, about 20 miles north of Aberystwyth for the following six weeks or so. It was here that we began our training as anti-aircraft radar operators on the somewhat antiquated 3 Mk 7 Fire Control sets. In 1958, there were no enemy aircraft so we practised with a Mosquito towing a drogue.

During this time, we were also introduced to personal weapons, namely the trusty .303 Lee-Enfield No. 4 rifle and the Sten gun, a worrisome and unreliable piece of kit.

Marching through the transport lines one day, a Blakey (steel plate) came loose on one of my boots, causing it to ring on impact with the ground. Our sergeant, a wonderful, hatchet-faced old boy coming to the end of his service, called the troop to a halt.

The sergeant asked who the 'blankety blank' musician was. When finding it was me, he made me march up and down on my own, singing 'Hi De Hi, Ho De Ho' at the top of my voice—followed by the rest of the troop for the next chorus. He surprised me later by thanking me for being a good sport in going through with this charade.

We all passed out of the course except one poor fellow with severe learning difficulties. And with the appellation of 'Trained Soldiers' we were sent on our way.

Bev Steele (Army)

I did my basic training at Carlisle—where I seemed to spend most of my time marching or dangling from ropes—and then was sent to Ridsdale Camp at Rhyl, where I was taught to drive 5- and 10-ton lorries. It was certainly different from my trade—I was a carpenter/joiner—but I enjoyed it. And, I suppose, I must have been quite good at it because, one time, my instructor fell asleep in the seat alongside me. So he must have felt reasonably safe.

Leonard Skipper (Army)

When I started my basic training at Catterick the food and accommodation were appalling. But then they transferred me to the Household Cavalry, to their base at Windsor. It was like a five-star hotel compared to my previous experience of Army life. The Household Cavalry serves two masters—it is a fighting unit, but there is also the ceremonial side. When I was in the regiment, it was a reconnaissance unit, with Daimler armoured cars. There are two sections, the Blues (now Blues and Royals) and the Life Guards. They put me in the Life Guards.

They asked me what I'd like to do and I told them I'd quite like to ride a horse, like some of the other men I'd seen at Windsor. I'd never ridden before, but they told me that, if I was serious, I'd have to sign on for an extra year. I thought about it. I was enjoying life at Windsor and so I thought I'd give it a go. I signed for the third year.

Derek Grattidge (Army: Household Cavalry)

Training for the Household Cavalry was not easy, particularly for a young man who had never ridden a horse before. Derek Grattidge, like the rest of the trainees, lived in barracks that were upstairs, the horses being stabled on the ground floor:

It was rigorous training, learning to ride, ten full weeks of it, all day, every day. Let's just say that at the end of the training you don't fall off your horse. And, of course, the horse was yours. You had to look after him. There were no grooms, you did it all.

After learning to ride, we were sent to Knightsbridge Barracks and that's where we learned the ceremonial side of the business—very important when it came to things like Trooping the Colour. Learning to ride was one thing, learning to do it in time with everyone else was something else again.

Derek Grattidge (Army: Household Cavalry)

After basic training in the Dering Lines at Brecon, I went into the Royal Signals, where I became a cypher clerk. All cypher clerks had to have at least one stripe to give them the authority to stop people—sergeants, officers, whoever—going into the cypher room. So they made me a lance corporal.

I waited for a few weeks for NCO training and in that time I was on constant fatigues, cleaning drains, boilers, and so on. Really, they were looking for things for us to do. They even hired us out to local farmers, potato picking. Back-breaking work, but the extra money came in very handy.

Then the course began. It was all about military law, fire arms, and things like that. We were drilled by three different sergeants; one of them was airborne, another was a Royal Marine. And they all taught drill in different ways. I think we got there in the end, but it certainly wasn't easy.

Haydn Burgess (Army)

The Navy, of course, did things differently. With a shorter period allowed for basic training, most ratings knew immediately what they were likely to be doing once they had completed their statutory period of bull and square bashing. Most national servicemen in the Navy ended up as writers, but some were luckier and were pushed into a specialised trade or department. A lot depended on what the man had done in Civvie Street, whether he had experience of the RNVR, and inevitably there were cases of being in the right place at the right time:

Because I was a member of the RNVR before I was called up, I was already trained as a seaman. So instead of going to HMS *Raleigh*, like so many of the other recruits, they sent me directly to HMS *Cambridge*, the gunnery school. It was very unusual to be given a specialist department and I was the only national serviceman in the intake. I was trained in exactly the same way and to the same standard as the regular sailors. It was a very intense course, from January to March 1958. When I left, I was classified as seaman/gunnery (Q), the 'Q' standing for quarters. It meant that I had been trained to be a member of a ship's gun crew.

Terry Colburn (Navy)

I did my basic training at the *Victory*. That was in September 1956 and I think I only did two or three weeks there. After that, it was by train to the battleship *Vanguard*, which was lying off Devonport—Britain's last battleship, she was then in Class 'A' Reserve—for a short course to finish off our training. She was lying alongside the *Anson*, a *KG5*-class battleship from the Second World War, and we used to cross to her to do PE on her deck at 6 a.m. every morning. We used to go back to the *Vanguard* in bare feet because she had wooden decks. We'd put our boots back on and go off to breakfast.

They decided to put the *Vanguard* in reserve at Portsmouth, so we were transferred to the shore base, HMS *Raleigh*. We were the first seamen to train there as, previously, it had been—and still was—a stokers training unit. That was the last of our training. When we finished at *Raleigh* we were sent to barracks, to HMS *Drake* to wait for a draft.

Jim Clarke (Navy)

Because I had finished my apprenticeship as an electrician before I got the call up—the papers dropped through my door two weeks after I qualified, would you believe—I was older than the other lads. And because of age and rank, they made me a leading electrical mechanic—I was the senior bloke right from go, even though I was national service. Not that I told anyone, most of the blokes I went on to serve with were regulars.

Training wasn't too bad. I was young, fit, and played rugby. I also tried boxing—once. A guy I'd become friendly with during training was a Scottish amateur champion. I used to box with him, sparring like. Then he persuaded me to enter this boxing competition. The bloke I was to fight was a great big, ginger-haired boy. You could see he was a fighter because he found it hard to breathe through his nose.

My plan was to slap him first, then take a dive. So the bell went, I charged out and hit him. He went down in a heap. He got up, but he was all over the place. I didn't knock him down again, but tried to keep out of his way and, in the end, I won on points. He caught me with one almighty blow, mind you. I couldn't get my teeth together afterwards.

I was pulled up next day for not saluting an officer. 'Don't you know the rules, son?' he said. I explained that I'd been boxing and couldn't turn my neck. 'Daftest excuse I ever heard,' he said. That was it for boxing—I stuck to rugby after that.

Geoff Lewis (Navy)

Because I was going to be an educational coder, helping young sailors with their basic learning, I had to take training to show me how to teach. This was done at HMS *Mercury*, a good modern set of barracks where most of the communications were taught. I was there for five weeks, part of the Devonport Division.

One of the things they taught us was blackboard technique—not something you naturally think of, unless you're a trained teacher. For the final exam, the Head of Birmingham Grammar School came down to officiate—I think he was well entertained in the Officers' Wardroom. Anyway I did a big equation on the board, talking about it and explaining what was going on. Afterwards, the head came up and told me I'd put up the example the wrong way round. It still worked out—and, more importantly, he didn't fail me.

Bob Jackson (Navy)

The great bonus for most national servicemen was that, once basic training was over and trade training had begun, they were treated in a far more humane fashion. It was as if they had gone through their ritual induction and were now fully paid up members of the club.

Reveille was now, usually, an hour later each morning. The extra hour in bed, albeit still in the long barrack rooms that always seemed to accompany national service recollections, was a welcome bonus to men who had been existing on a few hours a night. To their utter joy, they were now also allowed out occasionally:

You had two sets of uniform, your battle dress for general wear and your best blues. When you went off camp, you had to be in your best blues. You'd sign out at the guard house and then it was off into town. You were supposed to be back by a certain time, but there was a hole in the fence and if you were late that's how you got in. You'd make your excuses the following day—sorry, forgot to sign back in. Most of the blokes on guard duty were your mates anyway and they'd usually sign you in. And you always paid back when you were on guard—I must have signed hundreds of blokes back in.

Getting out for the night was always a bit hit or miss. I remember once, at Catterick, sitting on this big stone, waiting for the post. My mate Jimmy and I were keen to get into Darlington for a night out, but we had no money. Then the post came—a letter for me from Willie Lyndsey, the bloke who'd persuaded me to try for the RAF. And in it was a ten bob note. It was the money we needed for the night out. That's what you did, you were all in it together and you shared what you'd got with your pals.

Ian Norrie (RAF Regiment)

Accommodation was also far better in the training camps. The wanton destruction of their property by NCOs—smashing mugs, tipping uniforms out of the window, etc.—was over and that meant the money they were paid was now all theirs— in theory, anyway:

I was paid 28s a week, plus an extra shilling because I played table tennis for the unit. On pay parade each Friday, you'd march in, up to the table where the sergeant was sitting, and give him the last three digits of your service number. Mine was 923—ask any national serviceman and that number is the one thing they've never forgotten.

You got your money and straight away they took a contribution for sport back off you. In my case, they also sent 10s home to my brother who was running the family home. That left me with 18s a week to live on.

Alun Williams (RAF)

I was married three months before I was called up—deferred because I was finishing my apprenticeship as a joiner. I went into the Army in 1960, one of the last to be called up. My wife wasn't very happy, she knew the system was coming to an end and couldn't understand why I'd been called up, but I loved it. Money, though, was tight. They took a lump out of my wages and sent it home to my wife. I was left with about 10s a week and out of that I had to pay things for like sports fees and Blanco. Not easy.

Brian Wheeler (Army)

I was paid about 4s a day. But then, when I was in barracks at Plymouth, I heard that if you qualified as a shallow water diver you could get an extra 8d (eight old pence, that is) a day. Now I couldn't swim, but I reckoned I could teach myself in a week—they'd be bound to start with theory, I thought, and I'd master it then. So I signed for the course and made the declaration that I was a swimmer.

When I turned up on the first day, I realised it was all practical and that we were going in the pool that day. I came clean to the PO and he went mad. 'Right,' he said, 'ten lengths under water.' I put on the wet suit and all the equipment and down I went. I was okay to start with, but then the mask began to fill up with water. I panicked and shot to the surface. 'What's the matter?' said the PO, 'water in your mask?' I nodded and he put his foot on my head and pushed me back down.

The course was long and difficult. That first day was only the start. We went down in a deep compression tank—and that's frightening if you can't swim. In the end, only one of us, out of ten people on the course, passed. So I never got my extra 8d a day.

Bob Jackson (Navy)

The contrast between trade training and the sheer hell of what they had endured before made most national servicemen more than happy. It was like waking from a bad nightmare to discover that what they had dreamed about was exactly that, a dream. Suddenly, the prospect of spending the next two years in the armed forces did not seem quite so bad:

After a short leave, I was sent with some of my draft to Weybourne Camp on the Norfolk coast, to a radar school. It was March and we lived quite snug in snow-covered Nissen huts, a time of bright cloudless skies and freezing temperatures. We were told we were more students than soldiers and to concentrate on our lessons. There were scarcely any parades and there was a rumour that those who passed to go to the 47th Guided Weapons Regiment (Field) RA, just forming near Aldershot, might well be sent to the USA later that year—which proved to be the case.

Bev Steele (Army)

Both my brother and I served in the Navy. We'd both been in the RNVR and knew things like Morse code and basic wireless operating procedure. John, my brother, went in May 1953, I went in August. After basic training at Victoria Barracks (HMS *Victory*) both of us did communications training at HMS *Mercury*, the signal school. It was intense training, very well thought out, very precise. Each class was made up of just ten national service ratings so there was time for individual teaching.

John Mayer (Navy)

Occasionally, it was the sheer lack of preparation that surprised national servicemen. When George Moretta requested the Navy at his initial medical and interview, he had been pleasantly surprised to be accepted. Most of his friends and acquaintances from Liverpool were in the Army and that was where he expected to end up, but the Navy it was:

I'd always wanted to go to sea and, in fact, had nearly joined as a boy entrant. But when they offered me the standard jobs—stoker, writer, storekeeper, that type of thing—I told them I wanted to be an aircraft handler or a naval airman. To my utter amazement, they said that was fine, an aircraft handler I would be—after basic training.

The job was, to put it mildly, dangerous. We regularly lost planes over the side and several men got killed in the process.

I became the hook man, who had to run out and take the cable off the landing hook once a plane had come down on the deck of the carrier and then pull it clear. That would allow the plane to trundle up the deck once it had been freed and the next one in the line could come down.

Naturally I expected to be trained in the job. But, after basic training, I was sent to Portsmouth and we all trooped onto the flight deck of the *Implacable*. I remember waiting there, waiting to see what would happen. What happened was nothing. It soon became clear that you learned on the job. There was no formal training. This was December 1948, not long after the end of the war, and I guess there was still a flippant, shrug-of-the-shoulders attitude around. Whatever the reason, we received absolutely no training in the job.

George Moretta (Fleet Air Arm)

After NCO training, I went to Harrogate for training in how to use the cypher machines. It was the winter of 1946–47 and the snow was thick on the ground, up over the level of the windows. And, of course, the heating broke down. They gave us eight extra blankets each, it was that cold. We still had to mount guard over the camp, standing there, freezing, with our pickaxe handles. Goodness knows why, nobody could get within miles of the place.

Haydn Burgess (Army)

Pickaxe handles were all very well, but, once basic training was over and trade training had begun, men realised that they were now serious soldiers and, as such, were to be trusted with all the weapons and paraphernalia of war:

I think you tended to get a bit gung-ho once you'd finished your training, particularly after your rifle and Bren and Sten gun drills. I think we all felt ready for conflict, wherever it might be. I remember standing on the square and the corporal in charge addressed us. He said, 'You are now officially paid killers.' Amazing for nineteen and twenty year olds.

Gerry Evans (RAF)

As part of our training, we were used to working with live ammunition. I was pally with a lad called Jimmy Rutherford from Fife. This particular day we were meant to be charging a Bren gun position. Now the gunners were supposed to fire 'rapid' over your head, when you were at a distance, single shots when you were close. They forgot and stayed on rapid. There were bullets everywhere. I tripped and fell—and I'll never forget Jimmy as he kneeled by my side. 'Oh, Ian, are you shot?' he said.

Later, we were in the 3-inch mortar squad together. You had to clean up the area after firing, burn all the cardboard boxes that the mortar shells had come in. But someone had forgotten to remove one shell and it just took off with the heat of the fire. It fizzed away between us and, luckily, caused no damage. I think they had an inquiry into that little mishap.

Ian Norrie (RAF Regiment)

As part of the post-war defence against a possible Russian attack on the west, all bridges across the Rhine were heavily defended, hence the term BAOR (British Army on the Rhine). Infantry, motorised detachments, tanks, all manner of defensive artillery mustered for the purpose. For men like Arthur Ainger, a vehicle mechanic who now found himself stationed at several different towns of the Rhine, military hardware was still a wonder:

I was a mechanic, I knew nothing about guns, but as I was attached to the artillery I thought I'd better get to know something about the field guns—25 pounders they were—that we were using. A friend told me, just before going on a shoot, that if you looked carefully you could actually see the shells as the left the barrel of the gun. Of course I thought he was pulling my leg.

My friend shook his head. 'Come and watch,' he said. He made me stand behind the gun as it fired. And to my utter amazement he was telling the truth. I could actually see the shell shooting out of the barrel into the air. It was amazing.

Arthur Ainger (Army)

To most national servicemen, life seemed like one perpetual series of training exercises, particularly for those who were stationed in Germany. Officer trainees, however, had a rather different experience of training. For doctors like Bryan Griffiths, men who were already qualified in their chosen profession, there was little the Army could do:

After my six weeks of, what could you call it, watered-down basic training, I simply went onto the wards. This was in the Army Camp at Tidworth in Wiltshire, a massive great camp full of soldiers. There was no more training, I was just unleashed on the squaddies. I didn't stay there long, it was just to gain experience before I was sent off to join the 2nd/5th Regiment of Royal Artillery at Bulford Camp.

Bryan Griffiths (Army)

We finished basic training and I went home for a week's leave. Then it was off to Liverpool and the ferry to the Isle of Man for officer training. They put us through lots of different tests and problem-solving exercises, but it was a very different attitude and atmosphere from basic training, much more pleasant and polite. We had a warrant officer in charge and part of his job was to instruct us about speaking in public.

One of the exercises was to take a flight of men up Snaefell. They gave each of the would-be officers a compass and a map and off we went, taking it in turns to lead the flight. There was mist all around and we had to troop over fields and hills—a test of leadership, I suppose. But we made it and got back to the pub for a cup of tea!

It was still quite physical. They had us camping out on the beach sometimes, dressed in shorts and hob-nailed boots. We were made to run on the soft sand. I reckon most of us managed about six paces before we collapsed.

After three months, we all went in for an interview with the CO. I didn't think I'd made the grade as I found it all very tough. The CO said, 'Well, you haven't done all the tasks, but you've got a good sense of humour. So I'm going to recommend you for a commission.' And that was it, I became a pilot officer.

Brian Chaplin (RAF)

Trade training was over and postings to units and ships were quickly given out. Naturally enough, everyone hoped for a foreign station. In an age when foreign travel was still rare, it was, after all, one of the few 'perks' of national service. However, very few of the conscripts had really begun to think about the conflicts that were erupting across the globe and, in the months and years ahead, national servicemen would have a full part to play in dealing with these situations.

5

Trooping the Colour to the Cod Wars

The post-war conflicts involving British troops in the country's colonial possessions were part of the death throes of a once-mighty empire. For reasons that were not particularly clear—not then nor in hindsight—the 1950s and early 1960s saw an increasingly beleaguered Britain attempting to hold back a totally understandable desire for independence in numerous small nations.

Having recently completed their training—where they were bullied, screamed at, and subjected to mindless petty dictates—national servicemen might have been excused for having a degree of support for the oppressed nations. In fact, it was the opposite. Having been brought up on dreams of empire, on the novels of G. A. Henty or W. E. Johns, and the notion that Britain was always right, whatever she did, most of them simply followed the party line. Following that line was what the hours of drill and the mantra of always obeying orders were all about.

For young men going abroad for the first time, it often seemed as if the stories of dishonest natives who would fleece soldiers as soon as look at them were all perfectly true. There was a constant feeling of superiority that seemed to fill the minds of most soldiers—civilians too—during the 1950s and 1960s. It was, in part, a hangover from the earlier days of empire, when Britain really did rule the world—and, of course, it was also one of the results of victory in the recent war, a victory that had been achieved, against all the odds, by British courage and British spirit.

This manifested itself into the general notion that no one could ever be as good as the British. No matter who they encountered—be they Korean, Malaysian, or even German—that attitude was always there. Sometimes, it even applied to other Brits:

There was a docks strike during my period of national service. We were based at Hornchurch at the time and they sent us in to unload ships—strike breaking, I suppose you could call it. We didn't think of the dockers, what they were trying to achieve, and while there may have been pickets we went into the docks in lorries, straight through. No workers solidarity there.

Michael Beddis (RAF)

In Cyprus, we saw the worst bit of the empire in action. It was the last dying kicks of the old system and many people felt they could behave as they liked. There was lots of drunkenness. The regulars resented the national service boys and the national servicemen looked on the regulars as sub-human. And some of them were!

The CO tried to discipline some of the RAF Regiment and so, in retaliation, the rest of the Rock Apes set fire to his trailer—presumably as an indication of their superior intelligence.

When French paratroopers arrived on the station, the Rock Apes welcomed them with open arms, mainly because they wore different uniforms and could be easily identified as suitable opponents for night-time fights in the NAAFI.

Reg Jones (RAF)

I always say the British Army didn't behave well in Germany. We were more like an army of occupation than equal partners in NATO. On manoeuvres, as we were motor transport, we always travelled at the back of the convoy, close to the Mess and the cooks. One night, the cooks all disappeared. They came back with dozens of chickens. They'd raided some poor farmer's hen house, stole the lot. No wonder the Germans didn't like us.

Brinley Robbin (Army)

I got on quite well with the Germans, but at night we'd have to patrol the base to stop them coming over the fence and stealing things like wood, equipment, and wire. They'd put planks of wood up to the fence and roll barrels of paint over them. God knows what they wanted with it all, but they'd steal anything they could get their hands on.

Ron Evans (Army)

When I was in Egypt, there always seemed to be dozens of kids—quite friendly until they reached about ten years old, when they seemed to degenerate into a shower of scroungers and hawkers.

Colin MacCallum (RAF)

I was in Cyprus when the EOKA troubles were at their height. We were targets, we knew that, particularly driving down Murder Mile in Nicosia. We didn't have much time for the Cypriots. Rag Heads we called them, not politically correct now, but it was all different back in the '50s. When we were doing airfield guard duty one night, sitting in a slit trench and waiting, some of them tried to steal rifles—they'd do anything to pick up a rifle or two. The sergeant told us to load live ammunition in the Brens. That was fine by us and so we fired over their heads, to frighten them. It certainly did that. You've never seen people run so fast.

John Williams (RAF Regiment)

One day one of Nasser's MIGs made a 'bold pass' on Akrotiri, but by the time we'd scrambled our fighters he'd turned and run. We heard later that the MIG pilot was so anxious to get back to Egypt that he'd over-revved his engine and ruined it.

Reg Jones (RAF)

In some respects, a recruit's first posting was as daunting as starting basic training. Men who had been away at public school probably had some sort of advantage over those who had just left home for the first time. They were used to the loneliness and the uncertainty of alien environments. For most of the new recruits, however, it was something they faced with trepidation. Going into any closed community like a barrack room or a Mess Deck for the first time was certainly not easy and, sometimes, it needed a bit of luck to start off on the right foot:

I was at the barracks at HMS *Collingwood*, waiting for my posting to the cruiser *Cumberland* to come through. When it did, a mate and I went out to celebrate. It was a terrible night, rain hammering down and we got soaked. They wouldn't let us in the night club because we were so wet and so we sat on the steps drinking whiskey from the bottle. We spent the night under a car, trying to keep dry. And then the car drove off. The commissioner saw us and thought we were dead—we were, dead drunk. He called the police, the military police.

I came-to in jail, in a cell. And as I was due to leave for my ship that day I was taken on the train by two military policemen down to Plymouth. There were two women sat opposite and I was crammed in there between these two big blokes. 'Where are you going, love?' one woman asked.

'Shut up,' said the policemen. 'He's not allowed to talk to anyone.'

'You bloody big bullies,' said the woman.

It was dark when we got to the gangway of the *Cumberland*. They put me into the paint locker and I spent the night, just sat there. Next morning I got a right rocket from the PO and was sent down to the Mess Deck. Everyone clapped as I came in. They'd heard of my exploit. It was the perfect start for me; I was accepted right from the beginning.

Geoff Lewis (Navy)

When you arrived at your base, your camp, you had to get signed in. You were given a card and it was supposed to be filled in by the officers or NCOs in charge of each section, to confirm who you were. It was, I suppose, some sort of verification. On the card were questions like what was your religion, what sports you were interested in, and so on.

Alun Williams (RAF)

When I arrived at my first camp, I went to get signed in. The radar section was based below ground, in a basement, and you got to it by lift. While I was waiting to get my card signed, a friend told me what had happened to him when he'd done the same thing. He'd pressed the button to go down, but the lift went up. So he pressed again. Up, down it went and then, inside the life cage, he saw a pair of boots, then an arm with stripes on it, and finally a very purple, angry face. He'd been sending the flight sergeant up and down. He was put on a charge, straight away—and he'd only just arrived.

George Best (RAF)

Most people accepted their postings with equanimity. It was possible, however, with a bit of luck and the wind in the right direction, to alter things in your favour:

In my list of preferences for postings, I put the Far East (Singapore) first, the Middle East (Cyprus) second, and Home (Germany) third. I got Cambridge. My mate was posted to Lincolnshire, which suited him as he was married and that was his home area. Off I went to Cambridge where they were training pilots to convert from propeller driven to jet aircraft. Interestingly, we had a lot of Iraqi pilots there.

There was a bit of ill-feeling towards these Iraqi officers and our CO issued an order—we had to salute them, regardless of how we felt.

Anyway, out of the blue I got a letter from my mate in Lincolnshire. They were closing his camp and he'd been posted to St Athan in South Wales, miles away from his home and wife. 'How do you fancy a swap?' he asked. It was sensible as Cambridge was close to his home and he could travel between there and the camp quite easily. We were both SACs, both had the same time left, and were the same trade, but everybody said we'd never get it. Even so, he made a request to his CO, I did the same to mine, and lo and behold the exchange posting came through. He went to Cambridge and I ended up in Wales.

Gerald Evans (RAF)

Sometimes the slightest accident could affect a posting and men who had been intended for one destination found themselves somewhere totally different:

I was hell bent on going to sea, not being stuck in a 'stone frigate'. So I applied for every sea-going posting there was. I was knocked back several times, but at last I got a draft to a cruiser heading for the Far East. I was delighted, but then I had an accident and ended up in hospital. The ship left without me.

The drafting commander said, 'It's clear you can't handle big ships!' He was joking, thank goodness, and he sent me to HMS *Pelican*, a frigate that was just off for an eighteen-month cruise along the coast of Africa.

Trevor Pickering (Navy)

Army uniforms were rough and unpleasant to wear. The boots, in particular, were uncomfortable, great heavy things that clattered when you walked and made your legs feel like concrete. Any chance to avoid wearing them was quickly seized on:

When I was sixteen years old, I got a lump on the back of my heel. The doctor sent me to a consultant and he told me it was just a natural growth of bone that would, in time, disappear. In the Army, it started to be quite painful because of those boots and all the marching. So I went to see the MO—after giving the lump a good rub to make it all red and angry looking. I was immediately excused boots and, not only that, excused marching and guard duty as well. For all my national service I walked around in a pair of daps and never did guard duty, not once, in the two years.

Brian Collins (Army)

Guard duty was something that everyone had to do—unless they were lucky like Brian Collins—regardless of their trade or rank. It was not something soldiers liked, mainly because it interfered with leisure time and almost always took place at night:

You had a rifle to carry when you were on guard duty, but no ammunition. You weren't trusted with that, so it was all a pretty pointless exercise.

I stopped an officer once. He was in his car and I was standing, freezing, at the camp gate. Next morning I found myself up on a charge—because I'd stopped him by holding up my hand, rather than with my rifle pointed, bayonet out and levelled at his chest. And, of course, I hadn't challenged him in the correct military manner.

Ron Evans (Army)

We did guard duty six 'til six, a long and boring time. We had about half a dozen guys in the cells, no trouble to anyone. So, as the corporal in charge, I let the guard off duty for the evening—on the condition they wouldn't hoof it and would come back at the given time. They did, but when the officer found out he went ape.

Gordon Denley (Army)

On guard duty you had a rifle and a short bayonet, a pig sticker as we called it. We'd sit in the hut until someone came along, then two of us would go out. One was the picket and he'd take the details of the guy wanting to come onto the camp, the other just held the bayonet.

Officers would come in in their civvies, but you still had to salute as a matter of courtesy. The picket would spot them coming and he'd bellow 'present arms' or 'attention'. One night, a guy said to me, 'Thank you very much for the courtesy, but you should be careful who you salute.' He was a corporal in the cookhouse.

Alun Williams (RAF)

For most of the newly trained soldiers and sailors, it was a case of growing up quickly. Like learning to drive a car—when you only truly learn to drive after passing your test—men found that there were two distinct elements in what was really a new educational process in the armed forces. Men learned to cope with and survive basic training before their real training or initiation into service life began:

We had to take our turn at the watch. Now the watch was divided into two, one part on deck doing seaman's duties, the other working ashore, either as shore patrol or as part of the 'Knuckling Party', which was, effectively, a riot squad just waiting for trouble. One night in Malta, we heard that twenty or thirty blokes were waiting to give a Scotsman in our crew a right hammering. He was a nasty piece of work that Jock, and we reckoned he deserved everything he had coming.

But late that night, we saw him coming along the jetty, quite happy—he'd sorted them all out. We were the 'Knuckling Party' and the Jock was clearly very drunk. We had to do something. 'Right,' said our petty officer, 'as soon as he gets on deck, surround him and on my command grab him.' Up the gangway he came and we dutifully surrounded him. 'Grab him!' ordered the PO. Nobody moved. We were all waiting for someone else to act first. He just glared at us and, in the end, walked through the ring and went below.

Terry Colburn (Navy)

We were on a NATO exercise and moored up at Mers-el-Kébir. This particular night I was part of the shore patrol. I wasn't aware of the significance of the place, but it was where the Royal Navy had shelled the French fleet during the war and caused lots of casualties. The French were still pretty bitter about it; after all, it was only 1949, just a few years since the incident.

We were very cocky, very sure of ourselves, and we paraded into the centre of the French canteen. The looks we got would have shattered ice. We visited a few bars and brothels to make sure our lads were okay and then we met our opposite numbers, the French shore patrol, outside the dock gates. They were armed to the teeth, guns, the lot. We had only night sticks. Their petty officer was legless, rolling drunk, and we stood there, watching them, wondering if they would shoot at us. They didn't.

I did get taken out to see the French Foreign Legion while I was there. They were a tough lot, mostly Germans, and came in dragging their rifles on the sand behind them. But I was so disappointed—they didn't have those handkerchiefs hanging out the back of their helmets.

George Moretta (Fleet Air Arm)

The armed forces in the post-war years were being slowly modernised; after all, the dropping of the atom bombs on Japan had ushered in a new style of warfare. However, for the first few years of peace, only the USA possessed nuclear weapons, so the national servicemen were trained and prepared to fight a conventional war.

In most cases, the work men had to do was hard and very physical. That applied whatever their trade, whatever particular service they were in:

I was with 29 Squadron, flying Mosquito night fighters. They became obsolete soon afterwards, but in the late 1940s they were still being used. The work was routine and physically very demanding. As an air wireless assistant, I had to wheel these big trolleys carrying radio batteries out to the planes and then lift them in. The radio was a great lump of a thing and the Mosquitos had a hatch in the underside. We'd have to lift the radio in and then bolt it in position. Sometimes we'd have to retune it as well.

Michael Beddis (RAF)

I used to love the Bren gun carriers. They were my favourite toy! I remember, once, giving my mate a race to the local café. He was in a lorry, I was in the carrier. I shot off across the fields and there was the road ahead of me, behind a bank of trees. Unfortunately, the road was higher than I thought and I couldn't get the Bren gun carrier up the bank. So I left it and walked to the café. I said to my mate, 'I'll need you to pull me out.' But we couldn't find the carrier—it had filled up with leaves coming off the trees. It was only when we noticed the damage to the trees and the banking that we realised where it was.

Arthur Ainger (Army)

The modern Army might be based around new weapons and equipment, but for Derek Grattidge in the Household Cavalry tradition was everything. The training was long, particularly when learning the ceremonial side of things. He was twice involved in Trooping the Colour and was actually on parade for the funeral of King George VI:

The state funeral of the King had been planned long before, like it is for all monarchs, but, even so, we did not have much time to rehearse. The day started with *reveille* at four o'clock. It was February and bitterly cold. We were in the quadrangle inside

Buckingham Palace and we sat there, on horseback, waiting for things to start. Some of the troop actually got frostbite, they couldn't move their fingers.

That day, as we went down the Mall, there were thousands of people gathered, five or six deep, at the side of the road. The silence was what struck you. When you were involved with Trooping the Colour there was always noise. Our horses were trained for it. But on the day of the King's funeral there was silence. All you could hear was the solemn beat of the drum, the clip of the horses' hooves and our band playing the Dead March. It sent all the hairs shooting up on the back of my skull.

Derek Grattidge (Army: Household Cavalry)

Derek Grattidge's troop officer was the Marquis of Blandford, later the Duke of Marlborough. During the time that Derek knew him, the Marquis had a very close relationship with Princess Margaret and could easily have wound up in the royal family, but, even so, there was 'no side' to him. He was, says Derek Grattidge, just 'one of the boys'. Other national servicemen also encountered well-known people:

Two guys I served with were Welsh rugby internationals. First there was Carwyn James. He was a bit older than the rest of us, having done his degree at Aberystwyth before coming in. He was a coder, if I remember rightly, listening to Russian radio messages. We used to sit and talk with him in the NAAFI at night.

Then there was Bryn Meredith, the Welsh hooker and, later, their captain. I think he actually got his first cap while he was in the Navy. I remember Wales playing France for the Triple Crown and when they won we were all out on the streets of Plymouth, celebrating for Bryn. We were singing 'Sospan Fach'—and I still don't know the words.

Gerry Evans (RAF)

I can't say I actually got to meet the Duke of Edinburgh, but I did meet his plane. I was at RAF St Athan and the duke flew in for some official business in Cardiff. Normally they brought their own crew to service and just check the aircraft. This time, for whatever reason, they didn't and so I serviced his Heron before the duke came back and flew out.

Larry Burrell (Navy)

I joined the Marines in 1949 as a regular, even though I'd been working on a farm and was, therefore, technically exempt from national service. I did twenty-two years with the Marines and became a weapons training instructor.

In my time I trained lots of national servicemen. Three of the men I trained stick in my mind because they all became well-known international rugby players. First there was the Scotsman Gordon Waddle, then Haydn Mainwaring from Wales, and lastly the English and British Lions outside half Richard Sharpe. They were all doing their national service and they all represented the Royal Marines.

Don Hooley (Royal Marines)

Several national servicemen who served in the Navy became involved in the first of the so-called Cod Wars between Britain and Iceland. The troubles began in September 1958, when the Icelandic government extended its Fishery Zone from 4 to 12 nautical miles. There was a later Cod War, but the first one lasted only a few months, ending on 12 November 1958. Altogether, thirty-seven ships and some 7,000 sailors of the Royal Navy were involved in the First Cod War. Among the men who took part in a series of running actions were the national servicemen Noel Smith and Stuart Ashdown:

I had an extended basic training because I broke my wrist doing the high jump and was confined in hospital for ten days. Then I was employed showing films—me and a couple of Wrens—in barracks for a while. But at last I was posted to HMS *Jutland*, a battle-class destroyer that was on the way to Rosyth for fishery protection duties.

I had two spells up there in Arctic waters, protecting British trawlers from the Icelandic gunboats that came out and tried to detain our fishermen.

Our Captain was a bit crackers, I think. Whenever he came across the gunboat *Thor*—or any other Icelandic ship, come to that—he'd sail around and around her, creating a whirlpool effect. Mind you, we were just as bad. When we came across Icelandic trawlers we'd stand on deck and throw potatoes at their crew.

Stuart Ashdown (Navy)

Our job on Arctic Patrol was to establish safe havens agreed with the trawler skippers to enable good-quality fish to be removed from the sea.

I was posted to the frigate HMS *Palliser*, a new ship that was found a bit wanting in the heavy seas up there. It was understandable; she was brand new and had never been tried in such waters before. You'd leave Rosyth and run straight into a Force 10 gale. The waves were huge and we had fixed lines on all decks.

Our only contact with the Icelandic sailors arose when we were hustling them out of our exclusive fishing zones.

Once our trawler men accepted that we weren't just weekend sailors, we had lots of discussions with them. There were lots of requests for assistance with nets that were freezing up or had got snagged in propellers. Sometimes our skipper might even loan them one of our divers to help with problems below the waterline.

Noel Smith (Navy)

Weather conditions in the North Atlantic and in Arctic waters were never easy, not even in the summer. Men who were on board the escort vessels during the Cod War were experiencing exactly the same conditions as those sailors in the Royal and Merchant Navies endured during the Russian convoys of the Second World War:

> The weather was terrible. If you fell overboard you had a few minutes, that's all, in the water before you froze. It was always cold—the wind seemed to come right off the ice cap.
>
> Once we picked up a trawler man who'd fallen ill and did a mercy dash back to Rosyth. It took us just thirty hours, which was pretty good in that weather. Our fuel tanks were as good as empty when we got there. But he survived.
>
> Stuart Ashdown (Navy)

> On rare occasions there would be a call from one of our trawlers to alert us of an Icelandic gunboat approaching. One incident I remember when the trawler men really didn't need our help. They were more than capable of dealing with the Icelandic sailors.
>
> As we came close, we saw the trawler men on their deck, chopping up fish and throwing the bits onto the decking, then encouraging the Icelandic boarding party to come across. All the while, the crew were making chopping actions with their large knives.
>
> Noel Smith (Navy)

> Quite often the trawler men would pass us over buckets of fresh fish. I was a bit older than most of the other lads and had a bit more idea what to do. So I'd pinch some potatoes from the galley and at night, in the engine room, I'd fry up fish and chips for the boys on watch. Fish and chips have never tasted so good.
>
> Stuart Ashdown (Navy)

The Cod War of 1958 was more a series of incidents than an actual war, but it was interesting for the young national servicemen. Other conflicts, in other parts of the world, were of an altogether more serious nature.

6

Sport and Leisure

Most national servicemen could have been excused for thinking that their two-year stint in the armed forces would be little more than an extension of basic training, a period in their lives when they were harried from pillar to post and the word 'leisure' simply did not seem to exist. In fact, once they arrived at their base, camp, or ship, they found that there was ample time for many different types of sport, entertainment, and leisure.

Life in the Army, Navy, and RAF was, by the nature of the tasks involved, very physical. So it was, perhaps, inevitable that 'the National Service years were ones of terrific inter-service rivalry at sport'.[1] If you were a sportsman of any skill or ability you could be sure of an interesting and rewarding few years:

If you enjoyed sport you could have a really good life in the Army. When I was posted to Singapore it wasn't long before I was playing football for the REME. At the same time, I was scrum half for my unit's rugby team. It wasn't just team sports like rugby and football, either. We used to go swimming off Changi Beach. It was absolutely beautiful as long as you didn't think too much about the anti-shark netting they had installed to keep the sharks from getting too close to the beach.

Ken Williams (Army)

I loved all sports and was always playing rugby. I was a centre and played for the regiment. The only trouble with that was that lots of the blokes I was serving with—and playing rugby with—came from up north. They were used to Rugby League, not Union like me. When you'd fall on the ball they'd kick hell out of you—'Don't hold onto the ball, then,' they'd say. Different rules, different game.

Out in Osnabrück in Germany, I came across some old, disused canoes and so we founded a canoe club. We had about eight in all and we used to practice on the canal behind the barracks. We went up and down the Rhine, which is a pretty fast-flowing river.

If we could, we'd hitch a lift with one of the Rhine barges, throw them a line and get towed against the tide. We'd always put our 'compo' rations in the canoes and whatever sweets and chocolate we had and give them to the kids on the barges.

If we were off on a long trip—and we did plenty of them—we'd plan it carefully. We'd send our trunks and tents on ahead and set up camp on the river bank. It was great fun, that canoeing club—shame it had to end, really.

Brian Wheeler (Army)

The facilities for sport were amazing, both in the Army and the RAF. On board ships, things were, naturally, a little less elegant, but in the larger land bases even the Navy catered well for its ratings. National servicemen and regulars used the facilities available to them, often starting an interest that stayed with them for life:

Wherever I was posted I made use of the sports facilities. In St Athan we had a gym, an indoor running track, weight training rooms, and a great heated swimming pool— it certainly all helped to keep me fit.

I loved swimming. When I was posted to the Persian Gulf, the pool, naturally enough, was in the open air. We'd finish work in the early afternoon and I'd often spend my free time in the pool. When I was first posted to the desert, there were barely 100 airmen on the camp and that meant I virtually had the pool to myself. Things changed later, when they sent large detachments of soldiers to the camp and then the pool seemed full of squaddies. But to start with, it was like having your own huge pool in the garden.

George Cheeseman (RAF: Regular)

I played rugby, on the wing, for the 7th Destroyer Squadron. Most of the players were officers and while there was a lot of snobbery—a 'them and us' type of thing—it didn't happen on the field. They accepted the other ranks as players, just like them.

While I was in Gibraltar I played football for the ship football team. And I even ran in the 4×100-metre relay while I had a broken arm still in plaster. Lots of the opponents weren't happy—they said the plaster made me run faster!

Stuart Ashdown (Navy)

Out in Cyprus I played football for Akrotiri station. This one day, we played a Turkish Second Division side. Several times I took the ball off their left winger. He got madder and madder each time it happened and then the crowd got on his back. They were calling him names and he was shouting back at them. In the end, he got so angry he leapt over the fence and attacked one of the spectators, a man who had obviously shouted something pretty bad at him. Next minute everyone was fighting and throwing things, a right proper riot, all around the ground. We were made to stand in the middle of the field, well away from the trouble, waiting for things to quieten down.

John Williams (RAF Regiment)

My main sport was football. I played for the regiment and that was a pretty good standard. We played almost every other day, against other regiments and local teams. And when we weren't playing we were training. I've never been fitter.

This one particular day we were on parade. This young officer was staring at me so I just stared back. I remember he had bits of growth, the first beginnings of beard stubble, I suppose, on his chin. 'Sergeant, put this man on a charge,' he barked.

'What for, sir?'

'Insubordination.' He must have guessed what I was thinking!

After we were dismissed the sergeant said, 'Forget it. You've just been volunteered to go and watch a football match in Wrexham, Northern Command against Southern Command. So off you go.'

It was a terrible day, rain hammering down. I was stood with my coat collar turned up, hunched down against the rain, standing on what looked like an old slag heap. Suddenly my name and number were called over the tannoy.

I went to the changing room and the trainer said, 'What size boots do you take?' They were short of players and I was being drafted into the team. They fitted me out with kit and the next thing I knew I was on the park. There were some big names playing that day, some of the best players in England, and I even managed to put a goal past Frank Swift, the Manchester City and England goal keeper.

That story stayed with me throughout my service life. So when they sent me to Germany, I went as a footballer. I was known as a good player and that really helped me to gain acceptance from the other lads.

Arthur Ainger (Army)

I did my basic training at RAF Padgate, and then got sent to Thorney Island near Havant. It was a Coastal Command station and I was a fitter/mechanic on the air-sea rescue boats. But the first thing I did when I got there was to join the station hockey team. I'd been playing hockey since I was about thirteen and I was soon a regular in the side.

Once, travelling through London for a match, we stopped off to watch the wedding of Princess Elizabeth and the Duke of Edinburgh. When was that—1947? There were thousands lining the streets.

Reg Gooding (RAF)

Most national servicemen were straight out of school, so they were young and fit, well used to team games like football. It was the same for university graduates and men on apprenticeships. Lots of them had played for college or works teams, so it was just a case of transferring loyalties, now, to the regiment or unit.

However, the call up meant that men of a sporting or physically active nature were now suddenly exposed to many new and different activities. For some of them, the sports on offer had previously seemed to be well outside their remit. They were games that they had never even considered playing:

In training, they found that I was a good shot with the old .303 rifle. In fact, I became a marksman. If nothing else, it meant an extra 2s a week in my pay. To qualify as a marksman you had to get a 4-inch grouping at a distance of 200 yards. It was no easy thing to achieve.

In Germany, I was attached to the 7th Armoured Division, the old Desert Rats. I was on the mechanical side, but they learned that I was a marksman and the next thing I knew I had been chosen for the Divisional Shooting Team. It was a team of ten, half of them officers, four NCOs, and me, the only squaddie. But they were great, very accepting. I was just one of the team.

We travelled all over Germany, taking part in shooting competitions. And when we weren't competing we were on the range, in the butts, practising. Great fun.

Brinley Robbin (Army)

After I got my commission I was posted to Melksham as a technical training officer. I did try to explain that I was a mechanical engineer and now they were expecting me to teach electricity and electronics. 'Don't worry,' said my CO, 'you can mug it up.'

After I'd been in for a few months, I said to the station commander that I'd been in the RAF for ages now and yet I'd never even seen an aircraft. He rang Duxford and arranged for me to spend a few weeks on a flying station. It was great. They had Hawker Hunters just lined up at the end of the runway, waiting for the Russians—who, luckily, never came. They took me up in a Meteor and we flew from Duxford to the Severn, then to Cheltenham, over my fiancée's house in Dursley. We even waggled our wings over my mother's house.

I even managed a test flight on a Javelin. What an experience. It was like getting a boot up the backside—you just roared straight up. We shot over a trawler, going through the sound barrier. I had a camera in my hand and, as the pilot nose-dived, it just floated up into the air and the strap wound itself around the handle of the ejector seat. We went up well over 30,000 feet, so high you could see the curvature of the earth.

And then I was introduced to gliding by John Dellafield. The moment I sat in the cockpit, before we were even towed up into the air, I knew this was the sport for me. It was something I really took to and, for a while, spent most of my weekends gliding. Even after I came out of the RAF, I was able to continue gliding at RAF Colerne near Bath. Gliding really was—and is—a great sport.

Brian Chaplin (RAF)

At RAF St Athan they had the University Air Squadron and they also had gliders. The only trouble was that the base was situated in the middle of the Vale of Glamorgan. It's flat, fertile farm land and, consequently, the gliders couldn't get much lift. So, although you could fly, most glider flights were of very short duration.

George Cheeseman (RAF)

In 1952, just as I was about to finish my national service, I heard that they wanted two clerks at Klagenfurt in the British sector of Austria. Both Austria and Germany were still divided into four states or sectors in those days—think Harry Lime and *The Third Man* and you've got it. Anyway, I really fancied some time in Austria and so I signed on for an extra three years. They made me up to sergeant and off I went to Austria.

I'd played rugby and hockey in school—in goal for hockey, a suicide position if ever there was one. But in Austria, I suddenly discovered skiing. Every chance I got, every bit of leave, I was on the slopes. I loved skiing—well, I loved everything about the country. At one of the depots where I was stationed you could hear wolves howling in the dark. It would put up all the hairs on the back of your neck.

I travelled around Austria quite a lot, skiing and walking, and just enjoying a very beautiful country.

David Lloyd (Army)

It was not just exotic sports like gliding and skiing that were on offer, Alun Williams had been a keen table tennis player long before national service, but now he discovered that he could indulge his passion as often as he liked—even if, sometimes, it did land him in trouble:

Two of us were sent for trials for the RAF Table Tennis Team. The other lad, an East End 'wide boy' called Ken, was very street wise. At least he seemed to be. The night before we went for the trials, he picked up our expenses for the trip down to London, but he blew it all on the dog racing. So there we were with no money to get down for the matches. I borrowed £2 from a WAAF I knew and as there was no other way we hitchhiked down.

We booked one room at the Union Jack Club, a cheap services club. One room, that's all we could afford. One of us slept in the bed, the other on the floor. And we were starving, we had no money to buy dinner or breakfast. We played in the Trials Match and, amazingly, got through to the second day. That second night we slept in the back of a parked lorry in a builder's yard. It was January and we were frozen.

We had no money, but Ken said we could get coins, enough to buy us a bag of chips, out of the old telephone boxes by tapping the bar. It didn't work so maybe he wasn't as street wise as he thought.

We didn't get past that second day—we weren't in any fit state. And it was midnight before we got back to the camp at Sutton Coldfield.

Alun Williams (RAF)

Service life provided young men with opportunities for personal growth and development, if they wanted to take them. It was very much left to the individual:

> I played a lot of football when I was in the forces. I suppose that took up most of my leisure time. But there were so many opportunities that I could—and, looking back now, should—have taken up. You could learn to glide or horse ride if you wanted. Out in Lunenburg you could even take a course and learn German. I didn't. I regret it now, but I was young—we all were—and I suppose we had other things on our minds.
>
> Ian Norrie (RAF Regiment)

Not everyone was interested in sport, however. Nevertheless, there was still plenty to do and no one could really complain about being bored, even though they were away from home and loved ones. For some servicemen, the sight and experience of foreign countries, foreign cuisine, and foreign culture were enough, for others national service provided the opportunity to learn new skills:

> I started to learn to play the accordion when I was at Donnington, my first posting after basic training. I thought it would be interesting to learn a musical instrument. When I was posted to Austria, my musical ability just took off.
>
> I actually played in an Austrian dance band for a while and had a great time travelling around with the musicians. I don't say I was the same standard as them, but I suppose I couldn't have been that bad as they kept me on.
>
> The Austrian Army was reforming while I was out there. Once we were taking stores to Gratz and, as we reached the barracks, a squad of Austrian soldiers came marching up the road. They were singing 'Lillie Marlene'. I tell you straight, I've never heard anybody sing like those Austrian soldiers. Wonderful, quite wonderful.
>
> David Lloyd (Army)

> We had a music centre on the camp at West Malling. I was really into classical music and had been buying records since I was six or seven. Dvorak's 'New World Symphony' was my favourite at the time. I used to go along and play records to my heart's content—a lovely way to spend your leisure time.
>
> Michael Beddis (RAF)

> We didn't get a lot of leisure time and if I wasn't kicking a football around I was probably asleep. But the summer of 1947 was very hot and we took the opportunity for a spot of sunbathing. One of the boys was very fair skinned, he couldn't stand the sun, so we made a tent for him out of beds and bed frames. Then we went off to play football while he lay there, asleep. Of course, the sun moved and when we came

back he was terribly sunburned—but in triangular stripes where the sun had shone through the bed frames. Poor bloke, he was in agony.

Arthur Ainger (Army)

I was a big jazz fan and had brought my trumpet with me. We formed a four-piece band. The prime mover in this was Richard Wilcox, later to become a BBC producer on Radio 2. Dick, at nineteen, played the most fluent Jack Teargarden-style trombone, plus piano and guitar. He got us a gig, goodness knows how, at a big top rank ballroom in Aldershot. We were to be the interval spot, the main slots being taken by a big band, still in evidence in those days.

On the way to the gig, my trumpet fell out of the motorcycle pannier and was crushed beneath an Aldershot and District bus. The mouthpiece was the only item that survived. I wanted the 30s gig money pretty badly and, fortunately for my finances, had learned a few songs. With much trepidation, I did a couple of numbers up on the stage, singing into a huge microphone.

The squaddies and their girls seemed to like it. At least we got out alive and were paid! So I became the vocalist for the band. We kept the band together all through our service, including time in Germany. We even made an LP record—still in my possession.

Bev Steele (Army)

In 1947, I was posted to the Canal Zone in Egypt. They sent me to an Ordnance Corps Depot in the back of beyond, Tel-el-Kebir. The place was full of German prisoners of war, waiting for repatriation. They were obviously men from the old Africa Corps. They wore light blue tunics with a big black diamond on their backs and they had the freedom to more or less go where they liked. After all, the war was over and they were just waiting to go home.

But those POWs put on the most wonderful concerts. I'd always loved music, but this was something special. They even flew in musicians from Symphony Orchestras in places like Vienna. I'd be sat there alongside all these colonels and guys in red tabs, all of us just enjoying the music.

Haydn Burgess (Army)

For many of the national servicemen, one of the greatest benefits of serving in different parts of the world (home or abroad) was getting out and enjoying new sights, sounds, and smells—an experience that was very different from the things they were familiar with back home:

I was a non-smoker, a non-swearer—in fact, I'd even been an assistant scoutmaster before I was called up. I came from a rural environment and didn't even know what the inside of a pub looked like. I pretty soon discovered that I was no good at drinking. I just couldn't keep pace with the other lads, my shipmates. So I just didn't bother trying. I tried my hand at other things instead.

When my mates were all in the bars, I was off sightseeing. As we went to places like Singapore and Australia it meant I saw some wonderful things. I didn't know if I would ever see them again so I took every opportunity I could. Brisbane, Sydney, Melbourne, Adelaide, I saw them all before I was twenty-five.

I was one of the few lower-deck ratings with a driving licence, so I became one of the ship's jeep drivers, taking the officers out to barbecues. I also drove some of them to the Olympic Games, which were being held in Melbourne.

I didn't get much money, pay being what it was, but I managed to scrape together enough to buy a ticket for the last day of the Olympics. I saw a few of the athletics events, mostly the relays and the closing ceremony of those 1956 Olympic Games.

Patrick Line (Navy)

When I was on the *Cumberland* we went on a showing the flag tour around the Mediterranean. We went to so many places—the Bay of Naples, Capri (where we met Gracie Fields), and Malta, among others.

We spent a week in Naples and I remember climbing up Mount Vesuvius and going into the crater of the volcano. That was strange and to someone who had only ever seen smoke and grime in the steel works at Port Talbot it was something that was way out of my range of experiences. I've never forgotten it.

I also remember going into the harbour at Messina on the island of Sicily. The *Cumberland* was a big ship with tall superstructure and there were overhead power lines across the water. I think we missed them by inches. I suppose the skipper and the navigator knew what they were doing, but I hate to think what would have happened if we had hit those power lines. We'd probably have blacked out the whole island.

Geoff Lewis (Navy)

We lived in tents at Cape Greco on Cyprus for about three months. It wasn't as bad as it sounds. This was during the EOKA troubles, but we would just walk along the cliffs, without a care in the world, to an empty beach and swim happily in the Med.

Limassol, mind you, was tightly controlled. Everybody knew there were lots of EOKA supporters around and, as an acting corporal, I was put in charge of a small group of 'adventurers' who wanted to go into the town.

We were all issued with Sten guns and a clip of ammo each. As my regular, Scottish, homosexual flight sergeant impressed on me: 'Instrucct your men Corrporral. Better a clean hond than a dirty woman'.

I was never sure where he thought we'd get the money to find a 'dirty woman'—as national servicemen we were only paid a few pounds a week.

Reg Jones (RAF)

Sights like the sands of North Africa and the Suez Canal—still as much a wonder of engineering as the Great Sphinx and the Great Pyramids in those days—impressed themselves onto the minds of the young national servicemen:

It was a lovely lorry ride down to Ismailia, about 58 miles, along the Canal—rows of green trees along the side of the road for miles on end—the lakes of the Canal, the Canal itself, and the sky were a really wonderful blue colour, while the sand was bright yellow ochre and there were fields of bright barley and green stuffs all along the way.

Colin MacCallum (RAF)

After a period in Germany, my unit was posted to North Africa, close to the town of Benghazi. One of the things we did was to build a dam across a dry wadi—it was said that when it rained heavily, the water rushed down from the escarpment and washed part of the camp away. This dam was supposed to stop that. I actually think it was just to give us something to do!

Opposite the main gate of the camp you walked up a slight hill, down the other side to a lovely sandy bay. It was our swimming pool. At every opportunity we were there at the pool.

Bryan Berry (Army)

Posted to Nairobi, I flew from Cairo on a BOAC flight, an old Dakota. Looking out of the window, it was all there below me—the city of Cairo, the Pyramids, the Sphinx. My father had been there during the First World War, so I was pleased to see it all.

We went on down calling at Wadi Haifa, Khartoum, Kisumu, and lots of other places. We skirted Lake Victoria and, again, I saw it from the air. Later, lots of my mates came down to join me, but they went direct in a big old York—the passenger version of the Lancaster bomber—and they didn't get to see half of what I did.

Haydn Burgess (Army)

For young men, most of them just out of school, such experiences were priceless and they would remember them all their lives. That, combined with a sense of pride that they would never have previously owned or acknowledged, made the experience of national service in the Navy, Army, or RAF a rewarding one:

As a writer, the naval term for a clerk—a job that lots of national service boys were trained for—I never went abroad during my time in the Navy. I didn't mind because most overseas postings, *circa* 1949, were for two and a half years and would have meant an extension on my service. I just wanted to do my time and then get back to my real life in Civvie Street.

Having said that, I was proud to be in the Navy. I was proud of its traditions and history. I was never miserable, never. I had no complaints.

Larry Burrell (Navy)

That way of looking at things, whether the man was serving in the Army, Navy, or RAF, permeated the attitude of most national servicemen.

7

The Demon Drink

If there is any common factor in the memories of men who did their national service in the Royal Navy, it has to be the daily issue of rum. The practise of issuing a regular rum ration was initiated by Vice Admiral Edward Vernon in the year 1740, all ratings and petty officers being given their 'tot' twice a day. Known as grog, after Vernon's nickname 'Old Grog'—he always wore a coat of grogram cloth when he was on duty on his flagship—the tradition of issuing rum, albeit reduced to just once a day in the Victorian Age, continued until 1970 and therefore all national service sailors would have had their share of the Navy's bounty.

The Rum Bosun invariably had two fingers on the inside of the measure when the rum was poured, which meant that there was always part of each man's allowance left over. This was a bonus for the Rum Bosun and, if he was generous, for the members of his Mess as well:

> The Rum Bosun was the man who went to collect the rum for the Mess. He was usually the senior able seaman in the Mess. He'd set off with his container, called a fanny, and he came back with it chock full of this tar-black mixture. He would then pour it into the containers for the men, each of them holding their mug over the fanny so that lots of it slopped back.
>
> Rum was the main currency on board ship. If somebody helped you or did you a favour, say if they did a watch for you or covered when you were late on duty, they were repaid by a sip of your rum. Sippers, it was called. There were also gulpers, given for a really big favour. And then sandy bottoms—in other words the whole tot. It was rarely given and I think someone would have had to commit murder on your behalf to get that one.
>
> Terry Colburn (Navy)

We had grog, of course. That was two parts water to one part rum. To get a neat tot you'd have to be a petty officer. They were supposed to drink it at once, in one go, but lots of the POs I knew bottled it, kept it for special occasions or just for the weekend.

It was powerful stuff, so a couple of swigs of that Navy rum and you knew it. Mind you, the POs were old hands; they'd been drinking the stuff for years.

Bob Jackson (Navy)

There were men in the Navy who didn't drink, just like there are in all walks of life. I admired them, in a way, because there was an awful lot of pressure to be like everyone else and drink until you were blue in the face. You could refuse your tot and get an extra 3*d* a day, but nobody ever did that, at least not in my experience.

If you didn't want your tot—if you were teetotal or if you were just unwell on that particular day—you shared your portion around the Mess, with your mates.

Terry Colburn (Navy)

I was Rum Bosun for our Mess and there was always rum left over in the fanny once I'd dolled it out. It was the way you poured it into their mugs, holding your fingers over the rim to displace the liquid and pouring over the top of the fanny so that some of the rum spilled and went back into the container. That was mine, my perk or bonus. I used to use it to bribe the blokes in the NAAFI or the cooks on board so that we could get extra rations for the Mess.

Geoff Lewis (Navy)

On big ships—cruisers, carriers, that type of thing—the Bosun would pipe 'Up Spirits' at 11 a.m. and the grog would be given out at midday. But when I was on HMS *Upton*, a Ton-class minesweeper, there were only about forty to forty-five crew in total. The leading seaman in our Mess was the Rum Bosun for the whole ship. The officers were very young and our leading seaman more or less controlled the whole rum ration. He always got far more than the ship was entitled to. He'd give the other Mess their proper share and we'd get so much we could hardly drink it.

The rum was kept in big earthenware pots, done up in wicker. It was kept under strict 'lock and key' and it needed the officer-of-the-watch to get the key and issue it to our Rum Bosun. It was all part of a ritual.

Terry Colburn (Navy)

The ritual of the rum ration was a huge part of naval life and tradition, but as most national servicemen joined at the age of eighteen there was a problem:

You didn't get your rum tot until you were twenty and, for most of us, that was a pretty big event. We all looked forward to it. All the boys in your Mess would give you sippers, to celebrate—and friends in other Messes, too.

I was in Malta, on the cruiser *Cumberland*, when I hit twenty. I was captain of the officers' ladder, the companionway down the side of the ship, saluting and presenting for all the officers coming on board.

On my birthday, my old PO said, 'Don't bother to turn to after lunch.' He knew what was coming, knew the state I'd be in after all the sippers I'd be given. Of course, I didn't take any notice of his advice. I was all right to start with, but then, standing in the sun on the upper deck, I suddenly started to feel unsteady on my feet.

I went down the ladder, thinking the shade would help. No chance. So I thought I'd better get below. And then the captain's launch came alongside. How I managed to stay upright I'll never know. I had to get off the companionway ladder and balance on the stanchion—and salute at the same time.

As soon as the captain and the other officers were past, I crawled up the ladder, got to the Mess, and managed to sling my hammock. I felt like death warmed up, as the saying goes. I was ill for a week.

Terry Colburn (Navy)

Birthdays were always well celebrated, particularly when you were at sea. Because I had finished my apprenticeship before I went into the Navy, I was entitled to my rum tot right from the beginning. But I do remember my twenty-second birthday. You could sling your hammock almost anywhere there was space, but that night, because I was so paralytic, they put me in the hammock store. I slept standing upright, propped up by all the hammocks, spent all night and most of the next day like that. I think they thought that if I lay down I might choke on my own vomit.

Geoff Lewis (Navy)

Of course, it was not just in the Navy that alcohol was important. Indeed for most national servicemen, drinking soon began to assume significant proportions. It was as much the companionship and the *bonhomie* of the NAAFI or the bar room as it was the taste of beer. However, for young men, just finding their feet in the world or, perhaps, consumed by homesickness, alcohol soon became a part of daily life:

I spent most of my Army time as part of the BAOR, the British Army of the Rhine, at Roberts Barracks in Osnabrück. In town, our local was a little pub *cum* café, a place called the Oxo Cube. The owner, *Frau* Reidl, was brilliant. She'd mark down our drinks on a beer mat and we'd settle up with her on pay day. We didn't have much money, but the regulars, who were paid more than us, often subbed us for a drink or two. Great comradeship.

There were always six of us in our group and we'd sort out any trouble for the owner. After shut tap, she'd fill up a big, two-handled saucepan and put that on the table in front of us. We'd drink our beer directly from that. Sometimes we'd be invited up to her flat above the bar to watch football on the television. Her husband liked us—we went to visit him when he was taken into hospital. So it was a good time all round.

Brian Wheeler (Army)

One Christmas in Japan, on the way back from Korea, one of the sergeants and I went to this little bar. How it happened I'll never know. I didn't intend to get drunk, but, between us, we drank five pints of port. I remember being in the road outside and I couldn't stand up. The Naval Shore Patrol picked me up and took me home—thank God it wasn't the Army, they'd have just thrown the book at me. I couldn't move for three days, just lay there being sick.

Gordon Denley (Army)

I spent sixteen months of my service in Antwerp, attached to the 2nd Tactical Air Force, doing movement control on the docks. My billet was on the Museum Strasse, right on one of the canals. So there were always lots of mosquitos.

We used to drink at a bar across the road, run by a French lady called Madeline. On the first Sunday of every month, she'd put up a barrel of beer, free of charge, and food as well. We were good customers. We slipped the waitress a franc every time we had a drink, something extra from us. I think she appreciated that. 'Hello Taffy,' she'd say whenever she saw us come in.

Brian Collins (Army)

Out in Cyprus we used to drink the local wine—not the best. But then the French Air Force radio controllers came to join us in our lonely posting out on Cape Greco. And they brought with them armfuls of good quality French wine. I think it would be fair to say that we enjoyed the company of those French boys.

Reg Jones (RAF)

On Boxing Day, I met the CO wandering down to one of the tent groups, with a huge bottle of aspirins—there must have been 350 in it. Several fellows hadn't been sober for three days. Some didn't show it much, but one fellow was staggering around camp, bottle in one hand, hanging limp or swinging straight from the shoulder, and a mug of beer in the other hand. He was wandering along, executing a sort of square dance—a Rumba Step—into just about every puddle.

Colin MacCallum (RAF)

We were involved in a NATO exercise, along with French, Dutch, and Belgian minesweepers. We even went up the Seine to Rouen and spent time there before going up the canal to Brussels and then to England, mooring just below Tower Bridge on the Thames. Wherever we went, the Dutch ship was supplied with huge amounts of good quality beer and they smuggled lots of it across to us. We had the stuff stored all over the ship, in our kitbags, everywhere.

Our final port of call was in Holland, right on the Dutch–German border. By now, the whole crew was in a state of almost permanent intoxication. When we left port, I wasn't relieved on the wheel—my relief was so pissed. I was still there eight hours later.

Half way across the North Sea, we ran into terrible weather and almost everyone was seasick. In conditions like that, the Coxswain normally took the wheel, but he was too drunk. He eventually arrived, still half-cut. I don't think the skipper was too pleased, but I left the ship for my demob as soon as we docked, so I never found out what happened to him.

Terry Colburn (Navy)

Alcohol was one thing that was easily quantifiable for young national servicemen. It was always far more difficult to try to get a handle on the things that really mattered to them, things like companionship and life-changing experiences:

I was posted to Fassberg on Lunenburg Heath, the place where Monty took the surrender of the German forces in 1945. It was pretty close to the Belsen Concentration Camp and some mates and I went to see the place. It was eerie, that's the only word I can use. Mounds of earth where they'd buried people, over 10,000 of them, and what they say about the birds is true—no birds sang when I was there.

John Williams (RAF Regiment)

We drove past the Concentration Camp at Belsen. You couldn't go in, but they stopped our convoy and we sat there in our lorries and just looked. It was very silent, that's the memory that stays with me. They say birds don't fly over the camp. I don't know about that, but I certainly never saw any birds or heard any sort of animal life while I was there watching. It was frightening, in a way.

Ian Norrie (RAF Regiment)

Close by our camp, near Dortmund, there was this huge internment camp. It was for displaced persons and was guarded by dogs and sentries with guns. I didn't think about it at the time, but camps like that were all over Germany, for people displaced by the recent war. I wish, now, that I'd taken more notice at the time, but, even so, it still shook me up to see guards patrolling and it made me think, what's the difference between us and the concentration camp guards?

Brinley Robbin (Army)

You made some good friends in the service. I suppose it was people being thrown together in adversity. I kept in touch with the friends I made, at least for a while. Then it dropped off to just Christmas Cards and then stopped. I often wonder if any of them are still alive.

George Best (RAF)

I think it was the people I met that made my national service memorable. I was in barracks at Kowloon, battery carpenter for the artillery. It was 1958. We had a Chinese man working with us, Mr Lee. He took me around, me driving the unit's Land Rover, him taking me down these narrow lanes. He knew the area, knew where to get wood and materials. But he was so humble. He always called me 'Sir' and was so polite. The humility was just amazing.

A sixty- or seventy-year-old woman used to sit on the balcony of the Gun Club and make clothes and things for the soldiers. She embroidered a silk table cloth for my mother and father. It cost $25 and in those days there were about 16 Hong Kong dollars to the pound. The craftsmanship was unbelievable, so fine and good.

Len Skipper (Army)

I was called up in May 1951 and after a few months things began to hot up in Korea. A week before Christmas, I found myself on a troop ship heading out to Asia. Eight weeks we were on that ship and I tell you, you could cut the air, it was so thick with all those sweaty bodies. We were in bunks, three each side of the standee. Being short, I always opted for the bottom one.

The trip out to Korea was incredible. The Suez Canal was just amazing. I remember standing on deck and watching all the Arabs in the desert, waving at us. We had to lay up and wait in the Bitter Lakes while a convoy came the other way, then on down the Canal we went. We called at Aden—a god-forsaken hole, that was. Then it was on to Singapore, Hong Kong, and, finally, Japan. For a young twenty year old it was mindboggling. I mean, how else was I ever going to see places like that.

Gordon Denley (Army)

One of the things that kept men going, when it would have been very easy to slide into despair and depression, was humour. Very often, such humour was self-deprecating and as long as men had developed the ability to laugh at themselves they could get by:

Out in Korea we had a Mess Boy, a little South Korean lad. He was always happy and cheerful, but one day—I still don't know what made me do it—I picked him up and dropped him into this enormous great bin of flour that we had in the kitchen. I fell about laughing, and the rest of the cooks. Not him. He was furious and chased me round and round the kitchen wielding this bloody great knife and dripping flour everywhere. I was laughing, telling him I was sorry, and running until I was exhausted, but he kept coming.

Alec Maxwell (Army)

Before I went to my ship, I had to spend two weeks working with a gunner's mate on the firing range. It was a course for petty officers under training and the gunner's mate and I were working the butts. The other bloke, the gunner's mate, was still 'bomb happy' from the war. He used to stick his head up—'You move faster when they're shooting at you,' he'd say. I don't know about that—twenty POs with machine guns all firing in your direction was quite enough for me.

George Moretta (Fleet Air Arm)

We were up on the coast near the Kiel Canal and by 5.30 a.m. we were firing at drones that were being towed across the sky by aircraft. We'd all been out 'on the pop' as they say the night before and the effects hadn't quite gone away. For some reason, we kept hitting the drone—quite an expensive process and not something that normally happened. Finally our Irish sergeant shouted, 'Get those Welsh bastards away, they're hitting the drone all the time. They're still pissed.'

John Williams (RAF Regiment)

There was never any doubt that national service gave men an amazing range of experiences—and that applied whether they were stuck in Aldershot for two years or somewhere exotic like Egypt or Hong Kong. The key was to have an open mind and take each new moment as it came. For some, the things they saw and did stayed with them all their working lives:

The thing that stays with me is the intelligence of the horses that we rode. They were so clever. Horses, like people, have their own individual temperaments. Some are naturally nervous, others more controlled. But they can be taught. Every morning we used to ride to Whitehall, to get them used to the traffic and it was amazing how quickly they picked things up.

Sometimes we had troopers banging dustbins so that the horses could get used to sudden noises and crashes, trying to spook them. Look at any parade of the Household Cavalry. The more nervous horses are always on the inside of the formation.

My horse was called Charlie. He was the only one I ever had, a beautiful black stallion. All Household Cavalry mounts are black and most come from Iceland. They have to be a minimum of 14 hands.

I went into the Civil Service when I finished my national service, but I often think I should have stayed on in the Army. Even now, when I watch the Trooping the Colour or some other piece of pomp and ceremony I get shivers down my spine. I love the sound of a military band; it still has the power to move me, after all these years.

Derek Grattidge (Army: Household Cavalry)

I was attached to the Royal Marines when I was working at the M'Tafa Hospital outside Valetta in Malta. The Marines were experimenting with ways and means of evacuating casualties from bridgeheads, so we did all sorts of landings and simulated attacks on places like Libya on the North African coast.

We did several trips across the Med and then came ashore into very arid desert conditions and landscapes. Once, we landed at the historical site of Leptis Magna with its Roman ruins—the guy on the gate wanted to charge us admission. It was so funny, almost ludicrous. You could imagine it being part of a satirical show.

I felt I was very privileged during my period of national service. I had been promoted to captain and, as an officer, I had a standard of living that would have been difficult to maintain in Civvie Street.

As a doctor I was, for the first time in my life, taking responsibility for people's health—without turning to someone for advice. I came across so many different illnesses for the first time. There were lots of psychiatric problems, young men getting very depressed and needing help and support.

I came across leprosy, too. Now that was a disease that had been eliminated in most of the western world, but I saw people suffering from it.

Bryan Griffiths (Army)

One of my postings was to a place called Little Rissington in Gloucestershire. It was a very active station and they were flying Vampire jets from the base—still in service then, but coming to the end of their days.

We used to walk to the local pub, which was more or less at the end of the runway, and they'd land these jets as we were walking. I don't think they did it deliberately, that was just their line in to the runway. They were noisy things and we could hear them coming. We'd just dive on the grass whenever one was close and wait until he'd landed, then get up and walk on to the pub.

Brian Swain (RAF)

I was out in Egypt in 1951, several years before the Egyptian Crisis blew up. Having said that, they were still shooting at us occasionally and you had to take care.

I was there for eighteen months and for the first half year I was working in the hospital at General HQ for the Canal Zone, at a place called Fayid, close to the Bitter Lakes.

There was lots of traffic on the Canal in those days—French ships going out to Indochina, our own boys off to Malaya, and, of course, general cargo vessels. Egypt wasn't particularly luxurious, lots of dust and sand and flies. I used to stand and watch the ships going down the Canal. As I had worked on Thames sailing barges, I was interested in the traffic and in the feluccas that the Egyptians used.

It was amazing to just stand there and watch as a huge liner or cargo ship passed by. You couldn't see the Canal and it looked just as if they were travelling across the desert. It was certainly very strange. I can still picture it.

John Cotton (Army)

Leave, when it came, was a welcome relief. Most men tried to get home, but if they were far away in the Middle or Far East that was just not possible. For those who had families, things like the birth of a child caused more than a few problems:

Every six months or so we had a fortnights leave. My wife was due to give birth and I went to see the major, asking him if I could delay my leave and then take it in time for the birth. He agreed, but when my wife went into labour and I went to see the chief clerk, he said, 'He hasn't told me anything about it.' By then, the major himself had gone on leave so I was stuck. Typical, I thought. I didn't see my son until he was three months old.

Brian Collins (Army)

I came home for the birth of my child. No problem with getting home or the birth, but when it came to getting back then there were real troubles.

There were engineering works on the line and I missed the Boat Train in London. I was told I would go out the following Monday so I went home for the weekend. Then I got a telegram telling me to report to Queen's Barracks in London on Wednesday 13th. But there was no Wednesday 13th. I sent a letter explain this and they wrote back giving me a different date. By the time it had all been sorted out, I'd managed to get an extra four weeks of leave.

Brian Wheeler (Army)

Very often, national servicemen found themselves in positions of authority, either as officers or as NCOs. It was something they had rarely experienced before unless, as was sometimes the case, they were products of public schools where the prefectorial system and Army cadet force had given them some insight into the command of men:

I was a bit older than most of the lads I was with when they sent me to my first posting, near Market Deeping, so when the Suez Crisis blew up they made me an acting corporal.

Before I knew it, I was on board a brand new Britannia aircraft on my way to Cyprus. We landed in Nicosia and the temperature was 102 degrees Fahrenheit.

They put us into trucks and sent us off to establish a radar site at Cape Greco on the southern tip of the island.

On the road through the Troodos Mountains, our convoy was shot at by General Grivas and his EOKA terrorists. The national servicemen around me all eyed me with distrust as I was wearing corporal's stripes. They all thought I was a regular serviceman. I explained I was really one of them and after that we got on fine.

Reg Jones (RAF)

I was asked to stay on after my two years were up, but I refused. I'd had enough. They even offered to make me up to sergeant. I was already a corporal—although a very reluctant one.

When they first offered me promotion I said no. I didn't want stripes, didn't want the responsibility. So they hauled me up before the CO and he just couldn't understand. He made it very clear, told me that if I didn't take the stripes he'd make my life unbearable. I knew I'd be having a dog's life if I didn't take them.

So I became a corporal. But staying on, sergeant or no sergeant was a different matter. So I took my demob and was back home in Cheltenham just before Christmas 1953.

Gordon Denley (Army)

Offers of commissions and upgrading to NCO rank were often made by the powers that be. After all, they had gone to the expense of training young, fit, and intelligent men—it would be a shame to lose them now. In the main, such offers were ignored or curtly refused.

8

Parades, Troop Ships and Jankers

With national servicemen engaged on duties all over the world, the sight of soldiers and airmen—or, in the dockyard town, naval ratings as well—was commonplace throughout the 1950s and '60s. Only in wartime was there a greater preponderance of servicemen and, of course, local businesses—bars, dance halls, and tobacconists, in particular—seemed to thrive on the presence of military personnel.

In places like Cairo and Hong Kong, the mere appearance of an Army uniform was often enough to spark a selling frenzy. Hawkers and 'lookie-lookie men' seemed to lie in wait for squaddies or matelots to appear, and then they would leap out to make a killing. Sometimes, it was not just goods that people were selling:

I took the opportunity to visit places of interest whenever we docked. When we were in Malta, lots of the boys just stayed in Valetta, in the bars and clubs. The Gut, of course, was famous. You'd be walking along and an arm would shoot out of an alley to grab you. 'Hello Johnny, I remember you from last year,' they would say. Of course you'd never seen them before in your life.

Terry Colburn (Navy)

I came up from the beach, had an ice cream, and chatted briefly with a nice looking Turkish girl. She asked me home to see some great photos so I went, for a laugh. Her 'home' was a high-roofed squalid room letting straight onto the street, with bare lathes on the ceiling, cracked plaster, broken chairs, and a blanket and sheet slung on a line across the middle of the room. There was a bed with feminine apparel scattered untidily on it.

She showed me her photos all right—one 10 by 8-inch nude of herself for a start and various others, no doubt calculated to raise my blood pressure—as well as a huge collection of photos of Army and RAF fellows. The big picture wasn't particularly like her and I said so, whereupon she lifted her blouse and bra to show me her breasts. I saw the likeness then.

She was pretty insistent, but I told her of my girl back home and that I didn't want any 'jig-a-jig'. I gave her a photo of me at Cardington in my 'best blue' for her collection and escaped with my virginity intact. Aptly enough, her name was Virginia!

Colin MacCallum (RAF)

Bev Steele was a national service soldier who also played in a jazz band and he was often called on to play, both on the camp and out in public:

The band was popular and we entertained around the camp, previously a Luftwaffe fighter airfield about 10 miles from Dortmund. It was good to do this. It acted as a foil to the fairly tough activities laid upon us during the day. What with standing guard and gigging with the band, getting off camp to go down to Dortmund for a night out was a rare treat. Dortmund was a steel and coal town with chemical factories and breweries, a real working place where people knew how to party. I liked it.

It was good to take on a few beers on a hot night, meet girls—mostly students—at the ice rink and be amazed by their moves. I am talking skating here! I spoke a little German and was usually the one elected to order the beer and food for the group. There were soldiers everywhere at that time.

Bev Steele (Army)

The pyramids were disappointing at first sight, but when we got up close we could see just what a feat of engineering they are. We went into the King's Chamber in the centre of the Great Pyramid and saw the Queen's Chamber, too.

Down the hill from the pyramids was the Sphinx, with dozens of Arabs trying to hire out their camels and horses. We beat them down to 10 piastres and then they told us it was only the one way. We walked.

Colin MacCallum (RAF)

The one thing that all men who did national service had in common was parades. Whether they were in the Army, Navy, or RAF, parades were an important part of service life. Each day usually began with a parade and it was on the parade ground that the new recruits were 'broken in'. No matter where they were serving, parades continued to haunt them:

The band was playing 'They Locked Up My Darling in Allentown Jail'—a great favourite at the time. I was lead man and I just marched along, oblivious to everything, singing to myself. When the parade was over, the petty officer called me over. 'The Admiral enjoyed your singing,' he said, 'but not on parade, please!'

Geoff Lewis (Navy)

We were training to be cooks, but then the Army, in its wisdom, decided it needed us for the Queen's Coronation. Not cooking, just standing there. They wanted a soldier under every lamppost and on every corner. The number of parades we had for that, to practise standing still! And then, typical Army, they said they didn't need us, they had too many squaddies. And so they sent us to Germany instead.

Alec Maxwell (Army)

We went to Sweden on a 'showing the flag' cruise. We went to Gothenburg, then across to Amsterdam and Hamburg. And every place we went we had to line up on deck, all stood to attention. Parades? I was sick to death of parades at the end of it.

Stuart Ashdown (Navy)

In 1956, we were sent to patrol the west coast of Africa. One of our jobs was to hand over the naval base at Simonstown—a huge base just outside Cape Town—to the South Africans. We paraded and stood there while the Union Jack was pulled down for the final time. It had flown there above the dockyard for over 100 years. I found it quite emotional.

Trevor Pickering (Navy)

I suppose parading was part of our daily routine. Most people have seen the Household Cavalry on their horses, just sitting there on guard. Well, that was a parade, of sorts. At Whitehall we worked twenty-four hours on, twenty-four hours off. We were each given two-hour shifts—which are about all you can take, just sitting there on your horse, not moving or responding to the crowds. Your kit and the horse were inspected, minutely inspected, before you began your time on duty. It was all pretty gruelling.

Derek Grattidge (Army: Household Cavalry)

I spent the final years of national service at RAF St Athan in what is now the Vale of Glamorgan. When the station was given the Freedom of Barry, the nearest large town, in 1959, we had to parade and march through the town. It was a major celebration and there were thousands out on the streets. It was all best uniforms and shoe shine—I don't think my shoes had been so well polished since basic training.

Gerry Evans (RAF)

In the days before air travel became commonplace, troop ships were the easiest way of moving large bodies of soldiers about the globe. Many of these vessels were old passenger liners, now well past their useful life expectancy, but they were considered more than suitable for troop movements.

The use of old ships led to the occasional problem; these problems led to the occasional disaster, such as when the *Empire Windrush* sank in the Mediterranean in March 1954. The old ship—which had brought the original West Indian immigrants to Britain after the war—caught fire and sank while she was bringing troops back from the Korean War, many of them national servicemen. Luckily, all 1,276 passengers were taken off the doomed ship, although four engine room staff died in the disaster.

Most transits were carried out with a lot less drama, even though conditions on board were far from comfortable:

When things 'hotted up' in Korea, I was considered old enough to go (you had to be at least nineteen years old) and so, a week before Christmas 1951, I found myself on the troopship *Alladale* heading off to the Far East.

It was not a comfortable passage for most of the blokes. There were so many bodies down below you could walk on the air. *Reveille* was at 6.30 a.m.—imagine 400 blokes queuing for ablutions! So I quickly cottoned on that if I got up at 4.30 a.m., I could wash and shave before the crowd and be ready for breakfast at 7.30 a.m.

Eight weeks we were on that ship, the weather getting hotter and hotter by the day. I had been in the Sea Cadets and I'd have gone into the Navy for my national service if they hadn't insisted on three years instead of two. It meant that I enjoyed the time on the *Alladale*, despite the crowding. As far as I was concerned, it was a bit like a cruise.

Gordon Denley (Army)

I left Africa on Christmas Day 1948. Our troop ship was the *Ascaries*, an old Blue Funnel liner, coal fired and full of cockroaches. We were taken out to her in landing craft because she couldn't get close in to shore. First job was to find a bunk then line up for Christmas pudding.

We called at so many places on that trip home—Aden, Port Said, and others—but we couldn't get off the ship. I remember at one port a tug came out pulling two barges. They were full of what looked like coal. When they came closer, I could see that it was the heads of hundreds of native colliers, crammed in like pins in a cushion. They came alongside and started to coal the ship from barges. There was coal dust everywhere.

Haydn Burgess (Army)

We were on our troop ship, an Empire Line vessel, for nearly a month when we went out to Hong Kong. There were three other regiments, as well as our mob—the Battle Axe Corps as we were known—so it was pretty crowded to say the least. And, as we got closer and closer to Hong Kong, it got hotter and hotter. Everybody and everything, even the side of the ship, was sweating.

Len Skipper (Army)

Discipline is, perhaps, the other thing that most national servicemen harp back to when talking about their time in the services. 'The discipline did me good,' they say. It may well have done, but at the time the constant threat of jankers or being placed on a charge was on everyone's mind. Jankers, like fatigues, was not something anybody liked—after all, it interfered with valuable free time.

The term jankers meant a restriction of privileges for a minor offence where a serviceman had been put on a charge by an NCO. In the Army, the official terminology is CB—Confined to Barracks. In the RAF, it is Confined to Camp. Fatigues, a RAF term for boring, unskilled manual work, was not officially a punishment, but NCOs often used it as such.

During basic training, punishments were liberally handed out, supposedly being part of the 'bedding in' process. Even after men had finished their training and left for their first posting, the power of the NCOs and petty officers remained:

I hated gardening fatigues when we were put to do jobs like weeding and cleaning up the CO's garden. About six of us were set to weed his garden one day. I didn't have a clue about plants and despite constantly asking what this or that was I got no answer. So I just cut everything down. I think I destroyed his whole bed of daffodils. He was left with no flowers, just stalks and a few leaves. I never heard any more about it, so perhaps the CO wasn't too bothered about flowers either.

Alun Williams (RAF)

The only time I was ever on a charge came when I was at Catterick and tried to help out a couple of lads who had been put on general duties because of some misdemeanour or other. I was in charge of the ration store and early in the morning we went to the supply depot to pick up bread and other fresh food. These lads hadn't had breakfast, so I just cut off a few crusts and gave them to the boys.

A regimental policeman saw what I'd done and put me on a charge. I had to report to the guard room in full gear. The smartest dressed man on a charge was nominated stick trooper and allowed back to his barracks. I don't say I was the smartest there, but they seemed to think I was and so I was let off. Perhaps the officer in charge had some sympathy for what I'd done.

John Gibson (Army)

The Navy, as usual, had a rather different perspective on offenders. They certainly did not condone bad behaviour, but, unlike the Army or RAF, policing was done by the ratings and petty officers themselves. A man could be shore patrol one night and out with his mates the next—hardly conducive to impartial dealings with things like drunken ratings. Both the Army and RAF had police to deal with their troublemakers.

There was always a certain leniency towards men on a run ashore, particularly after they had been at sea for some time. It was when the seamen from other navies were ashore at the same time that trouble really began:

> When it was just the Navy in port it was usually fine. When the Yanks or the French were there as well, then you had trouble. There was fighting all over the place, in the bars, in the streets, everywhere. But the worst of the lot, I found, was the Canadian Navy. They were always terrible, wanting to drink and fight everyone. Then we'd gang up, the USN, the French, and us against the Canadians.
>
> Terry Colburn (Navy)

Most offences were minor in nature, often just flashes of temper or jokes that had gone too far. Sometimes, however, matters took on a more significant outlook and then the offence was clearly calculated with a goal in mind. Dennis Earle, for example, hated the Navy and stole a 10-ton yacht from Cowes. He intended to sail it to France and so escape the Navy's clutches. Arrested and convicted, he was sent to prison for 'the theft of the yacht'. Derek Kirby deserted, but, despite being AWOL for six months, spent all of that time hiding in the camp toilets and in a disused shower room and never actually left the camp. He stole food from the kitchens and regarded himself as 'a soldier living within my own unit'.[1] He was sentenced to six months' detention.

Clearly Earle and Kirby were in the minority, their offences notable mainly because they were so bizarre. For most national servicemen, the very idea of stealing a yacht or living alone, without friends or assistance, in an old toilet block were unimaginable. Even so, a man's character and temperament could and often did land him in hot water:

> For the first fortnight on the *Cumberland*, I was still on punishment for my escapade with a whiskey bottle and having been brought to the ship by two policemen. I spent much of those two weeks in Number 8s running around the top deck.
>
> You know, the word 'Taff' can be very aggressive sometimes, depending on the way it is used. This old leading hand was sat there, supervising me. 'Had enough, Taff?' he'd sneer. He was smoking, cigarette after cigarette. 'Had enough, Taff?' I looked at him and just shook my head.
>
> 'You'll die of lung cancer before I've had enough,' I said. He went ballistic and round I went again. And again! I already had a bit of a reputation, but after that it was even bigger.
>
> Geoff Lewis (Navy)

When we were going ashore, we had to wear our best No. 1s, our 'tiddly suits' as we called them. I was about to leave, when our leading hand, an old regular, suddenly pointed to a big hand print, in talcum powder, on the bulkhead by the door. 'Clean that off,' he said.

I hadn't put the hand print there and being a Scouser and about to go out, I retorted, 'Clean it yourself,' and off I went.

He must have tried the same trick with the next man and got a similar response because the next day we were both on report. The divisional officer asked if we'd refused an order in that way and we had to agree, we had. Our punishment was to clean the washrooms every night for a week. But he must have had some sympathy for us or thought the leading hand had over reacted because he was made to supervise us.

We were living in barracks. The leading hand lived ashore with his family. He'd have much rather been at home with them than being forced to oversee our work.

Larry Burrell (Navy)

Being on 'the other side', either giving out punishments or seeing them carried out, was also sometimes the lot of the national serviceman. It did not always endear them to their colleagues or friends:

Out in Cyprus with the Rock Apes I was seconded to the RAF Police who had a big wing in the regiment. We were responsible for the security of the front entrance to the camp, working with the Turkish Auxiliary police.

You'd have thought I had sold my soul to the Devil. All my so-called mates, men I'd worked and trained with, changed overnight. They called me everything, every vile name you can think of. That taught me something about people, I can tell you.

John Williams (RAF Regiment)

A lot of the trouble, when it came, was because of drink. I was on guard duty one night, in Osnabrück, and a load of blokes came back from town, clearly pissed. I asked for their ID, as I was supposed to do, and they refused. One bloke went to pull up the barrier so I rapped his hand with my pickaxe handle. After that they went quietly onto camp.

Our sergeant was sat in the guard house, watching the performance and after the blokes had wandered away he came out. 'Well done,' he said. 'If you'd have let him in I'd have had you on a charge.'

Brian Wheeler (Army)

I was working with a stores party down at Castlemartin camp in West Wales. One night I was fast asleep when heavy footsteps woke me up. The lights suddenly flashed on and there were two Red Caps standing above my bed. 'Get dressed,' they said, 'and come with us.'

I was clerk to the quartermaster at the time and when they started questioning me it transpired that the quartermaster had been selling off goods to the people of Pembroke, making himself a small fortune.

I knew nothing about his shady dealings, but they questioned me for ages. And then there was an ID Parade, a terrifying experience for an innocent man who knew absolutely nothing about what was going on.

David Lloyd (Army)

The commonly accepted view of national servicemen living and sleeping in long barrack blocks was not always the case, but that was certainly how they were quartered during basic training, in what were known as 'spider blocks'. These were long huts, each containing about twenty men, linked to a central wash area, exactly like the legs of a spider running off a central body. There were iron bedsteads, a locker, and that was about all there was in the way of luxury. Occasionally, men would live in 'spider blocks' throughout their two years of national service:

Most of the barrack blocks were made of wood. Ours was a bit different. It was brick built and looked just like a cowshed. So that's what we called the place, the Cowshed. The whole complex was built in the traditional spider style, lots of barrack rooms all leading to and from the wash rooms—which we all took turns at cleaning.

Alun Williams (RAF)

Privacy in such conditions was almost non-existent, but, if they were lucky, better accommodation might be waiting just around the corner:

In basic training we lived in the usual barrack blocks of the time. But when I was posted to Osnabrück in Germany it was very different. We lived in a four-storey set of brick-built barracks that had once been HQ for the German Army. There were just two of us to each room. So much space—it was like Heaven.

Brian Wheeler (Army)

Out in Cyprus I was billeted in Kyrenia Castle. I had an individual room—which was nice. It was, I suppose, one of the perks of being an officer.

The only trouble was the place had been a prison cell at some time. There were even bars across the widows. It didn't matter—the views were wonderful.

Bryan Griffiths (Army)

When I was out at Tel-el-Kebir in Egypt we lived in tents—six to a tent, if I remember rightly. I can still remember lying there at night listening to the sound of the crickets— there was greenery everywhere in that part of Egypt.

But then they sent me down to Nairobi in Kenya and from there in a convoy to Mogadishu, where there had been riots and public disturbances. It took us ten days to get there in our trucks and Daimler armoured cars and by then the trouble was all over. It was the journey that was special. We'd bivouac beside the vehicles each night, lying there under the stars. It was quite an experience, sleeping out there in the desert.

Then, when we got to Mogadishu, they posted me to a place called Gabrendare. It was so small it wasn't even on the map. It really was the back of beyond. Roads had petered out long before I arrived at my new base.

Apart from me and a REME sergeant, the only other British person in the place was the senior civil affairs officer, Lt-Col. Collingwood. We used to live in a wooden bando that was divided into three—a storeroom, a bedroom for the sergeant, and one for me. Water—which was for drinking and for washing—was delivered once a week and sometimes tasted of petrol. The weather was so hot you almost melted.

I was half asleep one night, curled up under my mosquito net, when I saw a snake slide in under the door. I nipped out of bed, got my Arab boy—a sort of general factotum who I paid to do cooking, washing, and other jobs—and he moved the furniture around until he found the snake. He killed it.

A massive spider dropped onto my bed one night and then, another time, something hit me in the chest—through the mosquito net. We searched for ages and couldn't find anything. Then the boy held up the sheet and there was an enormous great bat.

Haydn Burgess (Army)

I spent my last year at RAF St Athan in Wales, about 12 miles outside Cardiff. They had just held the Empire Games—forerunner of the Commonwealth Games—in Cardiff and lots of the athletes had been accommodated at St Athan. They'd built beautiful accommodation blocks for them, all with individual rooms.

When the Games ended, the RAF took them over—and what did they do? They gutted the buildings, took out the individual rooms, and made barrack blocks out of them all. That's where I lived for my last twelve months in the service. Why they couldn't have left the buildings as they were goodness only knows.

Gerry Evans (RAF)

On-board ship privacy was a rare commodity, with men crammed into small spaces, often slinging their hammocks wherever they could. There were compensations, however, and sailors could always tell themselves that the officers were not much better off than them. Laughing at adversity had always been the sailor's way and sometimes, if they were lucky, there was the chance to look at senior officers and take a quiet chuckle to themselves:

On the *Cumberland*, when we were in the Med, we had to carry out this exercise, pre-wetting the ship. It was to all do with possible nuclear attacks and was a supposed way of dealing with radiation.

The ship had sprinklers everywhere and when the exercise started they'd go off—water everywhere. Of course we knew it was coming and so we prepared. The captain used to walk around in his bathing trunks rather than get his uniform wet. Of course he still wore his cap—he had to let us know he was still the skipper. We used to laugh—behind his back, of course—at this little fat man strutting around in bathers and cap.

Geoff Lewis (Navy)

Brian Chaplin was one of several national servicemen who applied for and then took a commission. In his case, he served in the RAF. Clearly he enjoyed service life, despite its rigid conformity and dedication to seeming irrelevancies such as bull. Sometimes, the things he was asked to do taxed his imagination and skill to the limit:

When I was posted to Melksham they gave me a group of Jordanian mechanics to teach. One of the things we had to do was get them to understand Pythagoras' Theorem. When I stood in front of them, explaining, all I got was blank looks.

Then I had a brainwave. 'Surrealist art, right?' Nods all round. I drew a right-angled triangle on the board. 'This is Marilyn Monroe, right?' Huge grins. 'What's her smallest measurement?' The answer came crisp and clear—her waist. Then her hips. So the angle of the hypotenuse in a right-angled triangle equalled her biggest assets, her breasts. It may not have been perfect, but they understood the concept.

Unknown to me the Wing Commander had slipped into the room and was watching. 'I really have to say,' he drawled, 'that's the most unusual teaching method I've ever seen. Still, if it works...' I was at Melksham nine months, but I don't think I ever had greater attention from my students.

Brian Chaplin (RAF)

Other national servicemen who were offered the chance of a commission decided it was not for them and turned the offer down, often to the amazement of the authorities. There were those who had not applied for it, yet still went to the selection board as directed. Some were told that, in no uncertain terms, they would have no chance of a commission, not through a lack of skill, but simply due to unfortunate circumstances (such as having the wrong accent):

I was detailed to go to various rooms, for tests and things. I didn't know what was going on, why I was even there. A Wren officer interviewed me—what did my father do, what sports did I like, what I did for a living before national service and so on. And then she stopped, a look of sheer horror on her face. 'You've got a Welsh accent,' she said. She shook her head. 'Oh no, there's no possibility of you getting a commission, not with a Welsh accent.' That was the first I'd heard about a commission.

As far as I was concerned, my future was already decided. When I finished my spell in the Navy, I was going back to the legal profession, which was what I'd been doing before I was called up. So I can't say I was particularly upset by her comments. To this day I don't know if that was just her prejudice or the general view of the Navy. It didn't matter, I just knew I wasn't going to stay on.

Terry Colburn (Navy)

I was told they were going to put me forward for a commission and ordered to report for interview. I was seen by a Wren officer who went through all my details. 'Would you consider a short-service commission?' she asked.

I shrugged, 'I've never thought about it.'

She tutted and stared at me, 'Well think about it now.'

It took me about three seconds. I hadn't wanted to be in the Navy in the first place and now, here they were, asking me to stay on longer! 'Listen,' I said, 'I can earn £33 15*s* a week in the Steel Works. El Dorado we call it. You can't come close to that. So, no, I don't want a commission.'

She couldn't believe it. She thought she was offering me the world and here I was, turning her down. Now, in hindsight, I do regret it a little, but you can't look back. I made my decision and that was that.

Geoff Lewis (Navy)

They were 'cherry picking' certain grades, people they wanted to stay on and take a commission. About six months before I was due to come out, I was sent for interview with the wing commander. He mapped out a career path for me and, to be honest, it sounded really interesting. So I became hell bent on staying in and taking a commission, even though my parents were against it.

The RAF gave you time to think things over and then, a couple of weeks before demob, I had an interview with a squadron leader. Right from the start it was clear that he was not interested in national servicemen and was quite snotty about people like me wanting to stay on. It put me right off and I kicked the commission thing into touch.

Gerry Evans (RAF)

Even for those who did take the King or Queen's Commission there was still a choice to be made as their period of national service approached its end:

> I decided I'd like to become air crew, even though it meant signing on for twelve years. I went to Biggin Hill for assessment and was on the point of signing. But by then I was married and my wife wasn't happy with the social life of the Officers' Mess. She certainly didn't want me to go for pilot training.
>
> I'd been offered a job in engineering, back in Civvie Street, and so I didn't proceed with my application. I was demobbed on 21 October 1959. Looking back, I think it was probably the biggest mistake of my life.

Brian Chaplin (RAF)

> I don't think I ever thought seriously about staying on in the Army even though I had a great time and saw lots of things I might never have otherwise seen.
>
> But my career, my future, was as a doctor and medical work in the forces was limited. So when my time was up, I just took my demob and began my career as a paediatrician. National service had been good, but it was not for life.

Bryan Griffiths (Army)

Officers or other ranks, national service was an experience that was there to be enjoyed or endured—it was not a life-time vocation.

9

Faraway Places with Strange-Sounding Names

Many of the young men called up for national service in the 1950s never actually left Britain. They quietly and happily served out their time, waiting for the real world to start again. However, for others, their two years in the Army, Navy, or RAF gave them the opportunity to visit far-off places that they had only read about in books or seen on the Pathé News at the cinema.

Out of all the postings available, Hong Kong was considered the plum. With a garrison of over 12,000 men, the colony was supposed to act as a buffer for any possible Communist invasion from Red China. Invasion was an unlikely event, however, as Hong Kong provided China with a more-than-useful commercial link to the western world. The Chinese might posture and shout, but, in the 1950s and '60s at least, the colony remained perfectly safe.

Singapore and Malaya were also much favoured by national servicemen. The thrust for Malaysian independence did put something of a damper on such postings, with guerrilla soldiers, trained and equipped to resist the invading Japanese, soon turning their attentions to ambushing and sniping at British service personnel.

Cyprus was thought of as a good, safe posting—at least until Archbishop Makarios and General Grivas began their own independence campaign. Meanwhile, Germany, flattened and devastated by Allied bombing in the recent war and now divided into two by the Iron Curtain, was not normally a popular choice of posting as Cold War tensions heightened and grew.[1]

Unpopular as it was, Britain's commitment to NATO and the relatively close proximity of Russian troops, stationed in East Germany, Hungary, and Czechoslovakia, ensured that a large number of national service soldiers served out their time with the British Army on the Rhine:

Along with the rest of my unit, I did guard duty in Berlin for a while. This was in the 1950s and, at that time, there was no Berlin Wall, just a lot of barbed wire and frontier posts. We were armed with Lee Enfield rifles, well out of date, while just 100 yards down the road sat the Russians with sub-machine guns and all manner of modern weapons. If anything had started we wouldn't have stood a chance.

Berlin was still pretty battered when I was there, lots of bombed-out buildings. There wasn't all that much to see, it was very dark and dreary. There were some bars and clubs that gave a little night life, but the general impression was one of grim coldness.

We were billeted close to the Eastern Sector and I remember seeing Spandau prison where Hess and lots of the other Nazi leaders were still being held prisoner.

John Williams (RAF Regiment)

I was with the 56 Rifle Squadron of the RAF Regiment and after training they posted us to Lunenburg in Germany. It was a big town, a military town, and the Heath—where Monty had taken the surrender in 1945—was just littered with the wrecks of tanks, British and German. I expect the scrap merchants made a fortune out of them all.

We used to go into Berlin every so often for a two- or three-week stint of guard duty. You'd go in by train, come out by aeroplane. Funny, really, as you got close to Berlin we were told to pull down the carriage blinds. I still don't know if it was to stop us looking at the Russians or stop them looking at us. You had five rounds of ammunition, loaded in your rifle, but what good that would have done I don't know.

Berlin was still a wreck then, but they were starting to rebuild it. We didn't have anything to do with the Russians—they had a strict 'no fraternisation policy'. Mind you, the ones we saw were not the cream of their army. Russia's a big place and lots of those boys were just peasants, so even if we had been able to talk to them I doubt if we'd have had much in common.

Ian Norrie (RAF Regiment)

I served with the Essex Regiment, having been called up in October 1952. My first posting after training in the Catering Corps was to Germany. They sent us to Lunenburg, the place where the Germans surrendered. I was working in the Sergeants' Mess and spent the first few weeks getting myself used to Army life. Then, after six weeks, they turned around and said we were going to Korea. So I never got to see much of Germany at all.

Alec Maxwell (Army)

Lunenburg was a major base for the BAOR. Hundreds of Germans were employed in the various camps and barracks, and often British and German forces (and civilians) worked together on various projects:

I was with the Royal Engineers and went out to Germany on 11 September 1947. From 1 October to 18 December that year, I was involved in Operation Woodpecker, which was forestry work out on Lunenburg Heath. Our Sapper Unit worked with others to clear a site for a new road. It involved felling trees, digging up their roots, and levelling everything off. We built a wall of earth, using a bulldozer, while the fallen trees were rolled down an embankment, then measured and cut by German foresters.

Teams of horses pulled the trees away. They were led by Polish handlers—boy, those guys worked hard. The logs were taken away for use as pit props. All this axing and felling was done by hand—with occasional help from a dozer.

We also repaired roads across the Heath, laying what was called a corduroy road. In other words, logs would be lashed and laid down together, then secured with steel spikes. It was hard work, but rewarding as you could see the difference that had been made.

Bryan Berry (Army)

I was called up in 1948, originally for eighteen months, but before I'd done my time they extended national service to two years. I wasn't best pleased. They sent me to Hannover, to an Ordnance Depot as part of the Royal Army Ordnance Corps, the RAOC—it stood for 'rob all our comrades' they used to say.

I liked Germany and got on well with the people. I didn't smoke, but I still got a ration of 100 cigarettes per month. I used to sell them to the Germans at 10 marks a packet. They were desperate for them and it put a bit of money in my pocket. Lots of the boys in my unit weren't happy about that—they wanted the fags themselves.

Hannover had been pretty well flattened in the war. The centre of the place just didn't exist. I suppose because of the bombing, lots of the Germans weren't too fond of us and as we always had to go out in uniform we stood out like sore thumbs. I think it would have been a lot better if they'd let us wear civvies.

Ron Evans (Army)

I had a German mechanic working under me. Every Saturday I'd buy cakes from the NAAFI and we'd go to his house, share out the cakes and play cards. Willie, my mechanic, had a brother who was dealing on the black market, selling schnapps. One night it was blowing a blizzard, so I stayed later and later and we drank more and more of the brother's schnapps. In the end Willie had to carry me back to camp, through the snow.

Sometimes, when the weather was fine, Willie would drive around picking up all the odd bricks he could find. He'd store them in his back garden. 'One day I'm going to build a bungalow with these bricks,' he said. I lost touch with him when I was posted, but, do you know, I bet he probably did build his house.

Arthur Ainger (Army)

We had two NAAFIs at Lunenburg, one on the base, one in town. You could use either, they were both the same. And there were several cinemas, on camp and off. The Germans never used them, just the squaddies.

The troops always traded in BAFs, but, of course, you could only use them on the base, in the NAAFI. It was so many BAFs for a cup of tea, so many for a bun, that type of thing. It was Army currency and, I suppose, better value than the marks used off camp.

Apart from that, out in the town, there was a system of barter. I never smoked, but I got my allowance each month, like everyone else. Some I sent home, the rest I used to barter with the Germans for things that I wanted. I even had a photo taken by a German photographer and paid for it in cigarettes.

Ian Norrie (RAF Regiment)

In the 1950s, Hong Kong, Singapore, and Malaya meant a taste of the exotic East. Most large cities, London in particular, had a large Chinese community, a 'China Town' as people called the area where the Chinese lived and worked. Chinese restaurants were beginning to be popular, so to suddenly find yourself posted to a place where wonderful food and amazing sights were available every minute of the day was like a dream come true.

For any of the young men who had an interest and the imagination to appreciate it, the trip out to Hong Kong or Singapore was an experience and an adventure on its own:

They posted my regiment to Hong Kong, but before we went I spent days just crating up materials to be shipped out—probably officers' personal possessions. Then it was onto the troop ship, our regiment and a bunch of Gurkhas. The Gurkhas didn't like going below so they slept on deck. That was fine once we got to warmer climates.

We sailed across the Med and down the Suez Canal. We went so slowly down the Canal you could see the desert, vast and endless on either side of the ship. You could stand there for hours and just watch that desert. After we got through the Canal, we called into Colombo in Sri Lanka and spent a couple of full days there. Before we went ashore, boats full of hawkers and sellers came alongside, shouting up at the ship, all desperate to sell their goods. It was mostly cheap tat, but the sight of those boat sellers, dozens and dozens of them, is something I'll never forget.

We went into barracks at Kowloon. Hong Kong was like nothing I'd ever seen or smelled before. Even now I regard it as an educational experience. I learned so much and getting to know the Cantonese people was wonderful.

The heat I didn't mind, but the rain was just unbelievable. Driving through one of their storms, the water just kept coming at you down the gullies. It was like driving into a waterfall. You could easily have had your truck swept away.

I remember being on the ferry out in the harbour when a typhoon hit us. Up and down we went, like a funfair ride. Even the Chinese were worried. I came back in 1960, happy to be demobbed. It meant I could get to know my son—I'd hardly seen him. But I still remember my time in Hong Kong with great affection.

Len Skipper (Army)

SOUVENIR
PROGRAMME

VICTORY
CELEBRATIONS

JUNE 8th, 1946

PARISH OF LLANTWIT MAJOR

Chairman
Councillor W. H. WILKINSON

General Secretary
SAM ALLEN, Clerk to the Council

Organiser
Councillor LEONARD G. GREY

Price 3d.

Victory celebrations to mark the end of the Second World War were held across Britain. Following this came the task of picking up the pieces and helping people readjust, not just in the United Kingdom, but in colonial possessions too.

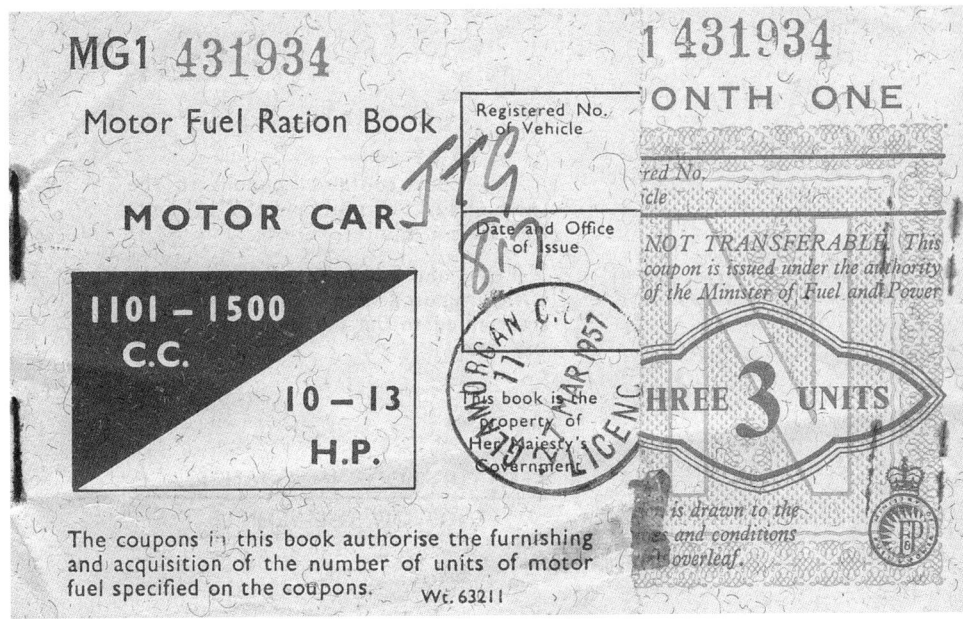

MG1 431934

Motor Fuel Ration Book

MOTOR CAR

1101 – 1500
C.C.

10 – 13
H.P.

Registered No. of Vehicle

Date and Office of Issue

This book is the property of Her Majesty's Government

1 431934

ONTH ONE

NOT TRANSFERABLE This coupon is issued under the authority of the Minister of Fuel and Power

THREE 3 UNITS

The coupons in this book authorise the furnishing and acquisition of the number of units of motor fuel specified on the coupons.   Wt. 63211

With the country virtually bankrupt, life in post-war Britain was hard. Rationing, for things like food and petrol, remained in place for several years.

Labour Prime Minister Clement Attlee—shown here with his wife—was the man who introduced peacetime conscription to Britain.

WHAT'S THIS "NATIONAL SERVICE"?

1ᴰ·

INDEPENDENT LABOUR PARTY
35, St. Bride Street, London, E.C.4

A photograph of a government pamphlet explaining national service and what it entailed.

A group of soldiers posing for the camera.

A photograph of Ian Norrie (second left) and a group of friends from the RAF Regiment.

A photograph of Colin MacCallum, newly drafted into the RAF.

A composite view of Catterick town and camp, where so many national servicemen were trained.

A photograph of Brian Chaplin as a new recruit, doing what all recruits did—polishing his boots. He was soon to go on to officer training.

A photograph of David Lloyd in Army uniform.

Physical education—or physical training as it was known at the time—was compulsory for all men. This group shot shows new recruits in the curious and unflattering PE kit they were forced to wear.

A photograph of Ian Norrie (second right) and a group of what he and others unflatteringly termed the 'Rock Apes'—the RAF Regiment, originally formed to protect RAF airfields and other installations.

A photograph of Colin MacCallum and mates at Compton Bassett.

Verne Citadel was the training base for the Sappers.

A group photograph of Royal Navy national servicemen. Geoff Lewis is fourth from left on the second row.

A photograph of Brian Chaplin, officer candidate.

A photograph of Michael Beddis (right) and the wireless section at West Malling.

A photograph of a Christmas party, December 1955. Colin MacCullum is seen here front left.

A photograph of George Moretta ashore on leave in Oslo.

An Army soccer team. Football remained hugely popular with all the recruits, being played wherever they were posted across the world.

National service gave young men the opportunity to experience new sports and past-times. Brian Chaplin, shown here in the cockpit, quickly discovered gliding.

For Brian Chaplin, it was not just gliding that he experienced in the RAF. This photograph shows him alongside the Javelin, in which he was given a flight.

Boxing was popular in all three services and in the Merchant Navy. This photograph shows two men engaged in a contest on board ship.

A RAF table tennis team pose with their trophies.

National service gave young men the chance to see the world. This photograph shows Sweet Water Canal, Ismailia.

H.M.S. "Cumberland".

HMS *Cumberland* was a veteran of the Second World War, but during the 1950s it operated as a trials cruiser in the Mediterranean.

A RAF parade at Catterick Camp.

The Sergeants' Mess in one of many Army camps in Germany.

Colin MacCullum and friend on sentry duty in Famagusta.

Units of the RAF are shown here on the parade ground.

New sights and strange experiences—Colin MacCullum and friend are shown here in front of the pyramids.

Brian Wheeler and comrades at Christmas dinner.

Brian Chaplin poses in front of a Gloster Meteor.

A photograph of the Somalia Signal Squadron. Haydn Burgess is seen here third from the left, second row.

A photograph of Ian Norrie and mates in Germany.

The huge NAAFI at Lüneberg, vastly popular with all of the troops serving in this enormous German base.

A photograph of Colin MacCullum and friend in a tent at Ayios Nikolaos in Cyprus.

A photograph of Brian Wheeler (second left) and a group of comrades.

A photograph of Henry Jones and his unit *en route* to Eritrea.

Henry Jones (centre) and friends in front of their vehicles.

A photograph of HMS *Veryan Bay*. The *Veryan Bay* was yet another Second World War vintage ship, which carried men like Bob Jackson around the world during their national service years.

The Panama Canal was an amazing experience for young servicemen.

A photograph of Bob Jackson and colleagues.

HMS *Upton*: a pen and ink drawing by John Morris.

HMS *Implacable* was a Second World War aircraft carrier that continued operating throughout the 1950s. This was the ship where George Moretta served out his time.

Hornets and Firebrands on the deck of HMS *Implacable*.

Operating aircraft from the deck of a carrier was a dangerous occupation. This shows a crashed Sea Hornet on the deck of HMS *Implacable*.

A Vampire jet on one of the lifts down to the hangars below deck.

Dockyard workers are shown here on a tea break—an apprenticeship in one of Britain's many building yards was one way of delaying the call up.

A Thames sailing barge—the men who worked these ships were also eligible for a deferment as long as they occasionally ventured out into the North Sea.

Coal mining, a dangerous, but highly skilled profession, also gave young men deferment from the armed forces.

A national service registration form that was carried by all Merchant Navy sailors.

A portrait of Bill Barker, shown here as an apprentice on his first trip.

Princes Dock in Glasgow, one of many teeming and busy British ports in the 1950s.

Cargo vessels regularly traversed the globe in the 1940s and 1950s, making the British Merchant Navy a huge and successful enterprise. This shows the *City of Perth* in port at Calcutta, one of many such vessels in use during the period.

David Sellars' Merchant Navy registration form.

A pen and ink drawing (by John Morris) of the *British Advocate*, one of many 'tramp' tankers that
were in use in the 1950s.

MILITARY CONDUCT _Very Good_

NOTE.—The Range of Military Conduct Gradings
possible is :—
(1) Very Good (2) Good (3) Fair (4) Indifferent
(5) Bad (6) Very Bad

Page 10
Army
Book
111

Testimonial. (*To be completed with a view to civil
employment and to be identical with that on page 8.*)

A quiet well behaved soldier
who gets on well with others.
Honest sober and trustworthy.
He always tries to do a
good job. A willing worker
who carries on by himself
and takes a pride in his
work. Cheerful and good
mannered.

Signature of CO

Date _19 Jan 60_.

Signature of Soldier

To be completed by the HQ, AER/TA Unit

UNIT STAMP

HEADQUARTERS

Depot Royal Artillery.

WOOLWICH

TERMINAL LEAVE
begins on _25 MAR 1960_
(the day following the reporting
date shown on Page 9)
and ends on _17 APR 1960_
both dates inclusive.

Signature of the AER/TA Unit

Date

LIEUT. COL. R. A.
COMMANDING DEPOT R. A

2 4 MAR 1959

(4895) Wt. 55628/4387 8/56 Hw.

The discharge papers of Len Skipper.

One of the curious railway trains that ran alongside the Panama Canal; they were an unfailing source of interest to Merchant Navy sailors.

The *British Advocate* was Ken MacCullum's first ship.

HMS *Jutland*, a battle-class destroyer.

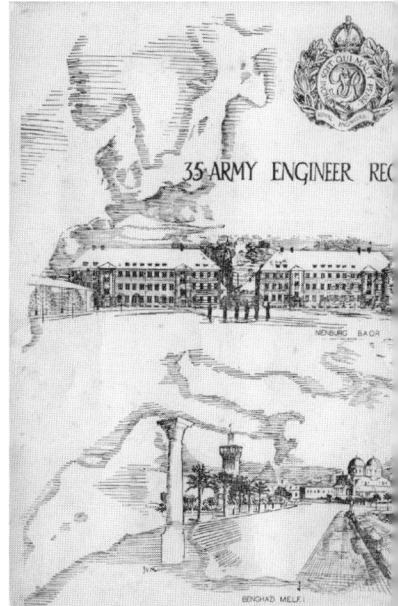

Above left: An exercise on Lüneberg Heath.

Above right: After demob, most men kept contact with their comrades only by sending the occasional Christmas card such as this one from the 35th Engineer Regiment.

As one of the first batch of peacetime conscripts, I went out to Malaya when the crisis there was in full swing. We were told to expect attacks at any time and so each of us was given five bullets to load in the magazine and five more in a packet, to use when we were on guard, if needed.

We were on the edge of the jungle, just a mass of green trees and bushes. All around the camp there was a 3-foot deep monsoon drain, great as protection I suppose.

There were always three men on guard, two walking around inside the drain, the other at the gate, stopping everybody as they came in.

We had Malayan soldiers with us as well. This particular night I noticed one of them sat in the hut alongside the barrier. He was sitting there and as I watched he loaded a bullet. He'd tied a piece of string to the trigger and before I could do anything he pulled it with his toe. Amazingly, the bullet missed his head and ended up in the roof.

Apparently his wife had been 'playing away' and so he decided to kill himself. It was just lucky he was such a bad shot. The MPs came and took him away and I never saw him again.

Ken Williams (Army)

I really enjoyed Cyprus, despite all the aggro from EOKA. The sun, the sand, their wonderful beer—brewed from onions, I think. We used to go swimming and catch small octopus. The Greek Cypriots would buy them off us, 2 old shillings each. We used the money to buy cans of cigarettes in the NAAFI.

One of the funniest things I saw was a French pilot who got into difficulties and ejected from his plane. We were on the fire truck and we rushed to get to him to see if he was all right. He wasn't injured, but he had come down near his crashed plane. 'Hey man,' he said, 'I've lost my lighter. Help me find it, will you?' A million pounds of aeroplane and all he was worried about was his cigarette lighter.

John Williams (RAF Regiment)

I went out to Cyprus in the autumn of 1958. At that stage, the emergency was still on and 2nd/5th Royal Artillery Regiment, who I was with then, lost a few men. We were only out there a few months when the London Agreement was signed and the regiment was sent back home.

The CO asked me what I'd like to do, go with them or stay. I was a doctor, not one of the gunnery officers and so there was a bit of leeway. I said I'd like to stay on, after all it was all part of the experience. I worked in the military hospital at Dhekelia for a time and then I was transferred to Malta. I was promoted to captain at the same time.

The hospital in Malta was a superb building, named after David Bruce, the man who discovered Malta fever. The architecture was outstanding, long and shady balconies and colonnades. When they sent me back to Cyprus in July 1959, I was sad to go, but there was no more work for me. I finished up as medical officer to the 1st Battalion

Royal Welsh Fusiliers, which pleased me as I'd had an uncle who served with them in the First World War.

Bryan Griffiths (Army)

When you went into Naples you'd tie up and the dock was virtually alongside the main street. We'd line the side of the ship, shouting and whistling at all the girls—who were doing just the same to us.

One of my mates, a Scotsman by the name of Fred, said he could drive. So we hired a car, a soft-top American thing. And we drove around Naples like we were kings. Then two police motorcyclists stopped us, pulled us over. Licence? We showed it. No good, it was a standard British licence. In those days you needed an International Driving Licence. That put us in the clink until we could get someone from the ship to come and get us out.'

Geoff Lewis (Navy)

One of the advantages of being posted to Cyprus or Germany was that men could take leave and visit other places that were equally as interesting. It was not something everyone did, but for those with the inclination such trips were a fascinating part of service life.

For a while, Colin MacCallum thought about trying the exotic city of Istanbul, but it was too difficult to arrange transport and so, with his time in the RAF rapidly running out and the troubles in Cyprus growing more dangerous every day, he was forced to look elsewhere:

Finally the CO signed leave chitties [notes] for five of us to go to Beirut. When we went up to Nicosia to collect our passports from the Emigration Office, we all had Sten guns. In all there were eight Stens and lashings of ammunition in the truck. I should think the driver felt safer than he had in weeks. We got our visas and went straight to the airport.

After landing in Beirut, we went to the dock area—it stank—along the banks of the river and then up to the better quarter of town—beautiful houses and hotels.

From the top of the hill we could see the whole of the Arab Quarter, all sparkling with lights, and more lights right up the hill and on to the other side of the river. The moon was almost full and we could see for miles.

The following morning, four of us decided to go by bus-taxi to Baalbeck in the Beqaa Valley, on the way to Damascus. It was a grand run up the mountains and over them into the plain of the valley where the Roman ruins were.

Damascus was much nicer than Beirut, to my taste—wider streets and not so congested. The souks were fascinating. Hordes of people all talking at once. Unfortunately it was Ramadan and all the shops closed at 6.30 p.m.

Colin MacCallum (RAF)

I was posted to a base near Dortmund. The town was pretty miserable just then, having been bombed and shelled in the war. And soldiers weren't allowed in some of the restaurants, whether by the Army or by the owners I don't know.

But there were compensations. Soon after I arrived, I was offered a place on a skiing trip the Army had organised up in the mountains. A couple of blokes had dropped out and they were looking to fill their spots. Lots of the boys couldn't afford it—it cost £6, which was cheap, even then. I jumped at the chance and was off before my kit was even warm in the locker.

Unfortunately there was no snow, so we couldn't ski. But the scenery was lovely and I enjoyed the evenings in the ski lodge.

Brinley Robbin (Army)

Standard postings were all very well, but many national servicemen found themselves in very bizarre and romantic places. Sometimes, the things that they saw were not very palatable:

I had two spells in Korea. The first time I had to come home because my father was ill. So after eight weeks sat on a troop ship, just getting there, and then a few weeks in South Korea and Japan they flew me home. The flight took five days in all, an old BOAC prop plane, calling at Tokyo, Okinawa, Hong Kong, Singapore, Colombo, and lots of European cities like Rome.

I was in civvies because we were flying over neutral countries, but I had no money so it wasn't a very easy time. What I remember most is sitting in the Mt Livinia Hotel outside Colombo and watching as the darkness came down like a shutter.

When I had seen to my dad, it was back on another troop ship and off to Japan again. I can still see myself, all on my tod, standing on the quay in Southampton waiting to board the SS *Devonshire*. She was a right tub, run by the RAF. Despite the condition of the ship, I enjoyed the cruise back to Japan—I was like a tourist.

Japan was nice, but to say it was a really different environment is an understatement. In the museum at Tokyo, they had the skins of Japanese men and women who'd bequeathed their bodies to the museum. The authorities skinned them and mounted them on the wall. Every part of the anatomy was preserved, to show various diseases I suppose. They even had Siamese twins preserved in a bottle. The guide offered to take us to lunch after that, but we declined!

We went to Hiroshima. This was, what, six or so years after they dropped the bomb and the place was still flattened.

The people were living in corrugated iron shacks. We saw some scary sights, people who had had their skin melted. It had run down their bodies and solidified. They were begging and it was pretty obvious they didn't have long to live.

Gordon Denley (Army)

We were posted to Nienburg, arriving there on 16 January 1948. Our very first job was 'squatting'—in other words members of the troop were sent out into town to find, sit in, and occupy certain empty houses. We then had to stock them with furniture—for the officers, of course.

Bryan Berry (Army)

The workings of the military minds that directed their lives were beyond most national servicemen. Sometimes it seemed that there was a way to do something, and then there was an Army or Navy or RAF way. In terms of postings, this was particularly the case:

I was all ready to go to Germany. My kit had been packed, my family informed, and I was given a forty-eight-hour embarkation leave. I came back from that and I was told that we weren't going to Germany at all. We were headed for Singapore and Malaya. Of course that meant lots of hurried letters—none of us had telephones at home in those days—to tell everyone our new destination.

When we got out to Singapore, we found ourselves in the main camp. I was REME, repairing dynamos, electrical equipment, that type of thing, so I moved around a lot. But my main base was Singapore. We were billeted just 100 yards away from the main War Cemetery where all the boys who had been killed during the Second World War were buried.

Ken Williams (Army)

We were training for Korea with the Welsh Regiment, but things got changed and we were rerouted. We joined the South Wales Borderers and were sent to North East Africa, to Eritrea, instead. It must have been about the beginning of 1951. There was something of an emergency going on out there, bandit activity by the 'Shifta' as they were called. We were supposed to put down tribal disturbances whenever they broke out—a sort of peacekeeping force.

We sailed out on the *Empire Ken*, an old German coal burner that had been handed over to the Allies in 1945, stopped at Algiers and then on, down the Suez Canal into the Red Sea where we docked at Massawa. They put us on a train, a diesel. There were still bullet holes in the sides of the carriages from a recent Shifta attack.

It was a strange country. You'd have these endless plains that seemed to run on for ever. And then, suddenly, huge mountain ranges. The capital was 9,000 feet up and to get there you'd be on tiny mountain roads with hairpin bends. Imagine driving a 10-ton truck up the side of a mountain. Going down was even worse, it was like dropping down a sheer cliff face.

They had this little narrow gauge train known as the Letrina. It had been built—like the railway line—by the Italians when they occupied the country before the war. It was a wonderful piece of engineering and when I was there in 1951 the carriages still had the Italian colours. Remember, there were no diesel engines like that in Britain at the time, we were still running on steam.

Henry Jones (Army)

My time out in Africa was an experience. It was like being back in the early days of the Raj. Mogadishu, when I was there, was a bit like a ghost town. There'd been rioting and about ninety Italian civilians had been killed, so there was a curfew every night. Even so, we managed to go swimming and I got stung by a jelly fish. It looked like a huge clear bubble trailing blue string behind it. Not a pleasant experience.

When I was posted to Gabredare, it was just me and my Somali driver, heading out into the unknown. I was really in the hands of that driver. I had the rank, but he had the knowledge and the experience of terrain like that.

One day, on the journey, he asked me if we could take a detour so he could see his family. I agreed and he drove us off into the middle of nowhere. We finally arrived at this village—dozens of villagers turned up to stare at me. They surrounded the truck

'Suddenly I heard a voice above the hubbub—'Good morning, sir.' I thought I'd been in the sun too long, but I shouted, 'Who said that?' And this little white-haired man shuffled forward.

'I used to be a sailor,' he said. It turned out he had actually lived in the docks area of Cardiff for a while and learned to speak English. I gave him a few tins of milk and we chatted until my driver came back from seeing his family and off we went again.

It really was an experience out of the Dark Ages, miles and miles of desert. There was no road to speak of and nobody in sight, anywhere.

We stopped one night at a wooden shack that was the home of a REME sergeant, whose job was to service Army vehicles in the area. It must have been the loneliest posting in the world for him. He had his shack with its veranda, but no company apart from passing squaddies like me.

The only way this sergeant could get around was in a massive Leyland truck with a crane on the back. His workshop was on the other side of the river and he used to cross it on a very rickety wooden bridge.

There were crocodiles in the river and I certainly didn't fancy falling in. I remember the rubbish dump by the river and the flocks of vultures circling the site, then dropping down for what they thought was a tasty morsel. To be honest I was glad to move on.

Haydn Burgess (Army)

Up in the hills—and remember, we were nearly 10,000 feet above sea level—there was a great risk of infection and so any cut or nick was always in danger of turning septic. You got used to it.

We had a soft—or softish—induction to start with, but things got harder after a week or so. We started with 1-mile or 2-mile march down to Asmara, but after a few weeks we'd go further afield, ending up doing perhaps a five to ten route march. You'd be surprised at the effect that thin atmosphere like that had on the lungs.

We had huge extremes of weather, especially heavy rain. There was light rain from June to July, then until September you had the heavy stuff. It was pretty barren up there where we were, but here and there you'd see the natives flailing corn in a patch on the side of the road—women mostly.

Henry Jones (Army)

For some lucky national servicemen it wasn't desert, heat, and flies that beckoned, but the bright lights of America. Bev Steele was one of a party of nine enlisted men (national service and regulars), plus officers and NCOs, who left Heathrow on a BOAC Monarch-class Boeing Stratocruiser in September 1959, bound for Albuquerque in New Mexico:

The other passengers were mostly wealthy Americans. It took us about eleven hours to reach Gander in Newfoundland, to refuel the aircraft, and to send a card back home to tell all that we had crossed the Atlantic, all very exciting and unusual in those days. Another two hours of flying time took us down to New York.

Two nights at the Grosvenor Clinton, a fine hotel built in the 1880s in Lower Manhattan, the mythical jazz joints in the areas of 42nd, 46th, and 52nd Streets all within walking distance. Seeing Count Basie at Birdland was, for this jazz freak, unforgettable.

It was then down to Albuquerque … driving across a seemingly endless desert road to our new home, a hutted encampment at a spot on the map by the name of Orogrande.

Bev Steele (Army)

Bev Steele and his companions were supposed to be testing guided missiles at the White Sands Proving Range. It was an exercise in co-operation between the British and American armed forces, but it was the side trips, events that took place once duty was over for the day, that made the experience unforgettable:

We managed to fire five missiles, one having to be destroyed, exploding spectacularly down range owing to a fault. A few of us, foolishly perhaps, took walks in the fierce afternoon to experience the sheer extremeness of the place, finding a few rattlesnakes and tarantulas on the way.

New Mexico was remote, seeming to be miles from anywhere. It had a strange, moon-like landscape with cactus and tumbleweed growing everywhere. It was very cold at night, but over 100 degrees Fahrenheit in the day. I remember the spectacular night skies, stars down to the horizon. And then the shooting stars that raced like tracer bullets arcing across the heavens. I never tired of that.

The trips we took in our off-duty times were exciting—car trips to El Paso, crossing over the Rio Grande to Juarez, a wild border town in Mexico where just about anything went. We had organised bus trips to Carlsbad Caverns and to a low-rise Las Vegas. It was a very remarkable month and our return flight to Blighty in early October was on the new Bristol Britannia.

Bev Steele (Army)

The Army and RAF might have had their moments, but as far as seeing the world was concerned those lucky men who had been taken on by the Navy regularly set off to experience life on the other side of the globe:

Our overseas commission began in February 1956, moored in the Pool of London alongside the Tower for four days. After that it was down to Simonstown in South Africa. On the way, we called at Gibraltar and at St Helena—we saw a tortoise that had been living there when Napoleon was imprisoned on the island.

Simonstown was a huge naval base. They had a massive dry-dock there, built to cater for the First World War ironclads. All around the walls they had the coats of arms of every ship that had ever docked there over the previous fifty or so years. That was pretty special, I must say.

After that we cruised up and down the east coast of Africa. We went to some strange and out-of-the-way places, saw people in dreadful conditions. We were 'showing the flag' and what we saw was really the dying stages of the British and French Empires.

Then, in October 1956, we received a message: 'Commence hostilities with Egypt'. We were all excited—it meant we were going to fire our guns in anger at last! We sailed up the coast, practising firing all the way. But by the time we got to Dar es Salaam it was all over. So we never did get to fire our guns in anger and it was back to boring sea patrols.

Trevor Pickering (Navy)

In 1956, I was sent out to the Far East as part of a draft to commission the *Cardigan Bay*, a Bay-class frigate. But before we reached her, we went to Mombasa to pick up the *Crane*, another frigate that had been badly shot up in the recent Egyptian campaign. It was the sort of thing that often happened, one posting or draft being altered or amended as the Admiralty saw fit.

When we reached the *Crane*, we saw that she had rocket holes in her deck and a Bofers gun on board had blown up, causing a lot of damage. She even had a crumpled bow where she'd rammed or hit something pretty hard.

We got to her at the beginning of December and sailed her, carefully, to Trincomalee—the Admiralty had sent her original crew home as it was thought they'd been through enough. We reached Sri Lanka on Christmas Eve, dropped off the *Crane*, and went on to Singapore to commission the *Cardigan Bay*, which we did in January 1957.

First off we went to Hong Kong, which was designated our home port, then on to places like Borneo and Port Dixon.

We were out in the Far East for eighteen months in all, taking in wonderful places like Australia and New Zealand.

We were actually seconded to the New Zealand Navy for three months and that took us to islands like Tonga, Fiji, and Samoa. They were just desert islands, really, very romantic and out of the way for young lads like us. I had never dreamed that I might get to see places like those Pacific islands.

After our time with the New Zealand Navy, we returned to Hong Kong for a mini-refit. We sailed out of Hong Kong with our Paying Off pennant flying and all the passengers on the liners in port stood and cheered as we went. We were lined up on deck, all dressed in whites, so it must have been an amazing sight. After that, we went to Singapore where we were paid off and I flew home.

Jim Clarke (Navy)

After my basic training, I was flown out to Singapore to join HMS *Cockade*, a steam-turbine destroyer. The port and town of Singapore were amazing, but I wasn't there long. The ship left Singapore on 2 November 1956.

We were escorting the Royal Yacht *Britannia* and sailed south eastwards into the Java Sea. They said, if I remember rightly, that the Duke of Edinburgh was on board the *Britannia*. We were only with her a few days, then we parted company. The *Britannia* headed south, for Perth in Western Australia, while we cruised on into the Flores Sea. We eventually went through the Torres Strait and down the eastern side of Australia. After that we spent weeks just 'showing the flag', calling at ports like Sydney and Brisbane.

Patrick Line (Navy)

Showing the flag was an important part of naval routine and activity in the 1950s and early '60s. It was a time when Britain still ruled the waves, when there were merchant ships and overseas possessions to protect. While many ships in the Royal Navy were Second World War vintage, they still looked spectacular to the people in the distant colonies:

I joined the *Veryan Bay* in January 1956. We knew we were heading for the Falkland Islands where we were to replace the *Protector* as guard ship and we knew we'd be away for twelvemonths. I was happy and excited. I came from a poor family and never went anywhere—the furthest I'd ever been was London for my interview as a coder. So the Falkland Islands? Just the idea of it was exciting.

Heading south we 'crossed the line' on 17 April 1956. Several of the crew had been through the ceremony before, but it was a first time for me—and I got the full works, being ducked and dumped and plastered with all kinds of horrible things. All part of the experience, I suppose.

One of our ports of call was Bermuda, a beautiful and quiet island. Walking through Hamilton town one day, a man stopped me and said that I looked like his son who had been killed flying in the war. He really looked after me, took me to lots of places, fed me incredible food and drink. On our last day there, he presented me with several huge bunches of bananas. We had been prohibited to even touch the things, which were growing wild out there, but I smuggled them on board and shared them out with the lads.

Bob Jackson (Navy)

Rules about picking bananas were one thing, but in places like South Africa there were more disquieting prohibitions:

I found myself on the wrong side of apartheid on several occasions. Once I was trying to send a card home and, for some reason, found myself in the wrong queue. This big policeman was suddenly stood in my way—'No whites here,' he said, and I had to go to the other side of the barrier. On busses we had to travel at the front, not the back and in some towns we weren't allowed to wear our uniforms. Some of those guys were still fighting the bloody Boer War. It wasn't good and lots of us found it hard to handle.

We had a group of Bantus serving with us on board, but none of them were prepared to work with the South Africans. When it came time to leave they just went home.

One of the Bantus got himself killed in a road accident. There was a terrible row— our skipper wanted him buried with full honours. The South Africans objected and said no way was that going to happen. The skipper just ignored them and we buried the bloke with full military honours, gun carriage—the lot.

Trevor Pickering (Navy)

I was made the ship's postman. All it meant was that the day before we made port I'd put up a notice on the daily orders, telling people what time the mail box closed. Then as soon as we'd tied up I was off ashore, looking for the nearest post office.

I couldn't speak any of the language, but it was pretty obvious what I was after. I did learn a few Spanish phrases and the like, just things like 'Post Office?' I'd deposit the bag of letters and cards and pick up any incoming mail for the crew. It was the same before we sailed. It meant I was first and last man ashore every time we hit port.

After we left Bermuda, we headed for Jamaica and then went through the Panama Canal. That was some experience. It took about twenty-four hours as there were so many locks to traverse. Going through the Suez Canal was boring by comparison. The

Panama Canal was impressive; you were so close to the sides you felt you could reach out and touch the rocks and cliffs.

We sailed down the coast of South America, calling in at ports and generally showing the flag. When we called in at one Chilean Naval Base, a plate in the ship's side split so we sailed in, grandly showing the flag, with a decided list to port.

Before being called up, I'd worked for the Elder Demster Line and so I told my mates where I was headed. One of the agents—and in those days shipping lines had agents in every port—arranged for a car and driver to meet me whenever we docked. That driver was to be available twenty-four hours a day to take me and my friends wherever we wanted. Even the skipper didn't have service like that—my mates loved it.

We didn't just stay in Port Stanley on the Falkland Islands, which was just as well as there were no docking facilities there then. You had to moor off and go ashore in small boats.

We were all over the place—Montevideo, New Zealand, even across to Mozambique and Freetown on the African coast. We really saw the world.

Bob Jackson (Navy)

When I came back from the Far East I went on leave, but, with the situation in Cyprus hotting up, I was recalled. I expected to go to a small, Ton-class minesweeper, but, instead, I was drafted to a fast motor boat. We only had a crew of nine and the skipper was a lieutenant. We were based at Cawsand Bay on the south coast.

That boat was a wonder. She was a fast estuary or river craft powered by three aeroplane engines. She used high-octane fuel, so there was no smoking on deck.

But on her I went all over the place, along the coast and over to Le Havre, Rouen, and we even took a long run up the Seine to Paris. She was shallow drafted enough to get away with all that. It was a lovely way to finish off my national service.

Jim Clarke (Navy)

The *Cumberland* was based in Malta, but on the way out we called in at Gibraltar. All the Spanish girls had to be in at a respectable time at night—unless they were ladies of questionable virtue.

It meant that lots of the boys were unlucky in their quest for female company— apart from one bloke who was boasting that out of the crew of 800 men he was the only 'successful' one. A week later he was found queuing up outside sick bay—he'd caught a dose.

Terry Colburn (Navy)

I was out in Malta for about nine months. We'd be out on exercise for a week or two then get back to the Grand Harbour and all the lads were ready for a night ashore. Most of us were well oiled when the ship's boats came to pick us up. So many of us lost our hats overboard and as for trying to climb up the gangway, God knows how we managed. More important, I'll never know how the guy on duty at the top managed to keep a straight face.

Geoff Lewis (Navy)

Wherever you went in South America you were entertained by the 'ex-pat' community. They'd come on board and we were always having cocktail parties and the like. One guy in Mar del Plata in Argentina, who had been on board for a party, decided he was going to give us a lift into town. The trouble was his driver had been entertained by the petty officers and he was well oiled.

It was a longish journey and once the driver swerved onto the grass at the side of the road. The guys in the front with him grabbed the wheel and set him back on course. Then he was across the road again. Luckily, this time he hit a road sign—just as well because if we'd missed the sign we'd have been over the cliff and that would have been the end of everyone.

Bob Jackson (Navy)

In January 1959, I left the *Cumberland* and joined HMS *Upton*, a Ton-class minesweeper—a very different experience from a large cruiser. We were part of the 100th Minesweeping Squadron, but we were an independent command so we tended to operate alone.

We operated, in the main, around the British coast, but we made trips, on exercise, to places like France and Belgium. It was a small crew, so there were only two Messes, a Seaman's Mess, which is where I was, and the other one, which catered for stokers, cooks, and so on.

After the Med, I found the seas around Britain a bit more 'lumpy'. When we came back from Holland, just before I was demobbed, I think everyone on board was seasick—so much for the romance of the sea.

Terry Colburn (Navy)

There are many stories of women found in every port, but it was just a myth, a legend, a tale told to titillate and amuse. Most liaisons between sailors and members of the opposite sex were brief encounters in back alleyways and of a decidedly 'paid for' variety. Unless careful precautions were taken, there was a very real risk of sexually transmitted disease that, apart from the pain and embarrassment, usually led to a loss of the rum ration for the rating concerned.

The mystique remained, however, and for national service sailors the dream was always a lot better than the reality.

10

Dangerous Days

Being called up to serve king or queen in the armed forces was, potentially, a lethal experience. Soldiering was, by its nature, something that very often placed recruits in various dangerous situations. After all, soldiers did get killed while on active service—death had always been something of an occupational hazard. Even so, it was not a possibility most men even thought about—at least until they were directly faced by the prospect of being wounded, hurt, or killed.

During the period that national service was in operation, there were conflicts in Cyprus, Egypt, Korea, and many other out of the way places. Aside from enemy action, the whole business of soldiering was an inherently dangerous one—accidents could and did happen on a regular basis.

It has been estimated that 395 national servicemen lost their lives on active service, while another 200 died from accidents while serving.[1] That might not seem an overly large number, but the fact that 600 young men (not counting those who were grievously wounded), who had no choice in joining the forces, died in peacetime was not something of which the armed forces or the government could be proud.

When disaster struck, it usually took men by complete surprise. Colin MacCallum found this out when the emergency in Cyprus suddenly began to assume greater proportions than he or any of his colleagues had ever thought possible:

The 3rd of September was, of course, the anniversary of the start of the Second World War. I was on duty. Just as I had logged in a failure of one of the radio circuits, there was a fearsome explosion. Plaster fell and bits of jagged stone came through the windows, showering glass everywhere.

Then someone started to scream. It was a horrible sound, bull-like and full of agony. I jumped to my feet and tried to look out of the window, but couldn't see a thing for the smoke and dust pouring in. I whipped out of the centre, but still couldn't see anything—and the screaming went on. I rushed forward and saw our Chiefie bending over poor Ali, the Turkish worker. He was half sitting, half lying, his overalls and face filthy, his eyes staring and bloodshot and his mouth was wide as he screamed.

His left foot was a mockery of a foot, blue bone showing through the mashed flesh and there was blood pouring all over the floor. As I stood, more or less stunned and horrified, there was another explosion and the place jumped in front of my eyes and under my feet and brown, dirty smoke and small particles of rock smashed through the remains of the window and through a hole in the thick outer wall.

Colin MacCallum (RAF)

Part of the problem faced by British servicemen as the people of Malaya, Cyprus, and the rest struggled for their freedom was that they were facing what we would now call terrorist organisations. Insurgents or freedom fighters did not announce their presence by lining up in time-honoured military fashion with drums rattling and trumpets blowing, nor did they stand up to shoot and be shot at.

Invariably, the unexpected bomb or rifle shot was the first that soldiers knew of the presence of their enemy. Regardless of the moral issues, it was a hugely effective tactic:

As part of our regular patrols, we had to drive down the infamous Murder Mile in Nicosia, so called because of all the ambushes and pot shots the Greek Cypriots would take at British soldiers. We were in open-topped Land Rovers, no protection from gun shots or bombs. We were just showing a presence. At the top of the street was the border between the Turkish and Greek communities. It was a bloody dangerous situation. I can't say any of us were particularly happy about it, but being there, driving down Murder Mile was just something we had to do.

John Williams (RAF Regiment)

By the beginning of February, there were almost daily occurrences of trucks being stoned and bombs being slung around. There was a riot by students in Famagusta and stoning of trucks again. A military police truck was stopped and stoned and while three of the four guys in it tried to get the truck started again, the fourth lad, one of our RAF Police, held off the mob by brandishing his Sten. This stoning got so heavy that he had to fire—just one shot. It sounds very British, cool, calm, and collected, but he probably just forgot to put the change stud to automatic. Anyway, he shot a student in the foot and that quietened the crowd.

More trouble in Famagusta next day, more riots and stoning, both of buildings and vehicles. A bomb was thrown at a truck near the Hadjihanlis Cinema. Fortunately, no one was hurt, but no one was caught either. Troops had to fire at a crowd in Hermes Street; one RAF policeman shot and killed an eighteen-year-old Greek student. All the shops closed in sympathy and the 200 civilian workers on our camp went on strike.

Colin MacCallum (RAF)

It was a stressful time for everyone, national servicemen and regulars alike. Nobody knew if it would be their turn next to be hit by a bullet or grenade. In hindsight, however, there were moments of light relief:

During the troubles in Cyprus, we had to mount airfield guard on the outskirts of camp. One night my mate and I were there, armed with Sten Guns and a couple of Webley revolvers. We knew that 'the powers that be' used to send out raiders, to try to get past security. It was to keep you on your toes.

In the Middle East, night comes down like a blanket and although we had one large spotlight it was only for use in emergency and so we couldn't see a thing. We heard sounds out in the darkness—maybe it was the blokes coming to catch us out, maybe it was EOKA. We listened. It sounded like grunting and there were bushes rustling and then the sound of coughing.

We issued the standard challenge: 'Come forward and be recognised'. There was no answer and so we opened fire. A couple of full magazines we let off—and we killed a wild donkey!

John Williams (RAF Regiment)

We were on our way out to Korea and called in to Hong Kong. While we were there, a tannoy message told us that an armistice had been signed. We all thought that would be it, we would simply turn round and go home. No chance.

When we arrived in Korea, we were immediately sent up to the front lines. Me and another guy were given this tiny tent and told to get our heads down. We tried, but all night long we could hear voices, Chinese voices. The 'enemy' was just a few yards away. It was frightening. After all, the peace had only just been signed and things could easily have blown up again. We were Catering Corps—God knows what they thought we could have done.

We were there, like that, for several days. It seemed like it was just us two against the whole Chinese and Korean Army. And it rained. I'd never seen rain like it. We were soaked. We'd get up in the morning, wring out our clothes and put them back on again. After a few days, they pulled us back and we went into camp about 10 miles behind the lines. I'd never been so relieved in my life.

I think the worst part of that experience was not knowing where we were, what we were supposed to do. Nobody told you anything.

Alec Maxwell (Army)

Danger from a hidden foe was one thing, danger from your own actions—or those of your colleagues—was something else. That did not lessen the fear or anxiety, but it did enable men to later laugh at their own foolishness:

Our admiral on the aircraft carrier *Implacable* was Philip Vian of HMS *Cossack* fame. He was the man who, in 1940, took his ship into the Norwegian fiord to rescue British prisoners on board the German supply ship *Altmark*. By the final years of the 1940s, he was the commander of our whole carrier fleet.

We had this new 'jumbo' crane and, as we left Portsmouth, somebody noticed that the hook wasn't painted. So I was detailed to get up there and paint it. It was the sort of thing we had to do every now and then.

Fine, heights didn't bother me, so I just sat in the hook happily painting away, say 50 or 60 feet above the water. My mate had me on a rope, but then it was dinner time and he just left me. I carried on painting.

I was suddenly conscious of a tall figure leaning over the front of the admiral's bridge. It was Vian. 'Do you want to go to a watery grave, sailor?' he said.

I shook my head, 'No, sir.'

'Then get on board until your mate gets back,' he said and turned away. I think that was the only time the admiral ever spoke to me.

George Moretta (Fleet Air Arm)

As well as being inherently dangerous, the bases to which national servicemen were posted were often historic. Longmoor in Hampshire, for example, had its own military railway line. Opened in the early years of the twentieth century, the line only closed in 1969:

I was posted to Longmoor, near Liphook in Hampshire. It was a great posting as, because of the railway connection, I could catch a train to Waterloo quite easily and then get home. But that railway also brought disaster.

We had this young linesman, a trainee. He let a train go down a single-line track. It was a 'down' goods train and it should, really, have waited because there was an 'up' train, a passenger train, approaching on the same line. Of course, they ran straight into each other.

It was dreadful. There were bodies everywhere. We had to carry them out from the wreckage in blankets. It was so sad. They held a memorial service for the victims. I shouldn't have gone because I was a Catholic, but I thought, 'Blow it, they need to be remembered,' and so I went along.

Brian Collins (Army)

When I was stationed at Ridsdale we had a really nasty accident. It was during a 'scheme', an exercise. One of the young national service boys pulled the firing cord on a field gun at the wrong time and the gun just blew up, exploded. There were two lads killed and several more injured.

I was driving a 7-ton truck at the time and I had to take the bodies to the station for transportation back to base. I can still remember the coffins being carried on the men's shoulders and lowered gently onto the train. It was all so moving.

Len Skipper (Army)

The troop ships we sailed on—going out to Africa and coming home—were not exactly the height of luxury. And to make matters worse, we hit severe storms, both ways, in the Mediterranean.

The ship was pitching and tossing, going all sorts of ways. And some of those troughs, you looked down into them and you would swear you were looking deep into the depths. Frightening. Things got so bad they could hardly stand to serve up food. Mind you, only two of us were in a fit state to eat the stuff.

Haydn Burgess (Army)

Apart from things like terrorists and troop ships, many of the jobs national servicemen were asked to do, like any physical or manual labouring, had a degree of danger involved. That was accepted by everyone, officers and other ranks alike. Support from colleagues, from officers, and NCOs was taken for granted. However, at other times, it seemed as if the military had little or no interest in the wellbeing and safety of the men:

I flew home from Cyprus in December 1956. I just missed getting on one of the famous Comet jets and, instead, had to fly on an RAF Hastings. The Hastings was probably the worst aircraft ever built. It was a terrible machine. It was so bad that only RAF personnel and Polish refugees fleeing Russian persecution were ever allowed to fly in it!

I was sitting next to one of the fuselage ribs. There should have been rivets every foot or so, holding the air frame together. But on this aircraft there were just two and I could reach out and rattle the whole rib. We touched down in Malta to refuel, but as far as I was concerned that landing couldn't come quickly enough—we'd lost one of our four engines an hour away from Malta.

We took six hours to repair the engine and then off we went again. We landed at RAF Lyneham on Christmas Eve and damn near crashed. There was a thick fog on the runway and we banged down so hard I'm sure the pilot hadn't been able to see the ground. He clearly wanted to be home for Christmas.

We were greeted by the congenial customs men, who rewarded their returning war heroes by smacking the maximum duty on all the cheap trinkets men had brought back for their wives, children, or girlfriends. They strip-searched one man—and, of course, the airman with the kitbag full of cigarettes was left untouched!

Reg Jones (RAF)

Reg Jones might have regretted missing his flight on a Comet, but other national servicemen certainly did not enjoy their experience of Britain's wonderful new aeroplane:

When I was called back from Korea because my father was ill, I started out travelling by jeep, then caught a big Gloucester transport plane. There were about 100 Canadians on board and the bloke next to me chain-smoked all the way from Seoul to Tokyo.

Once I arrived in Tokyo, I changed into civvies and found myself on board a Comet. I was excited—the Comet was the flagship of Britain's aviation fleet, supposedly a marvel of new technology and design.

Soon after take-off I needed to go to the toilet. Just at that moment, the plane hit an air pocket and dropped hundreds of feet through the air. I was standing in front of the toilet pan at the time and next thing I knew I found myself on my knees.

When I got back to my seat the guy in front was clearly terrified—and he was a pilot. Mind you, it wasn't surprising. When I looked out through the window as we took off I could see the wings wobbling and shaking. I didn't feel particularly safe on that aeroplane.

A few weeks later came the first of the well-recorded Comet crashes. And, of course, they resulted in the Comets being taken out of service. To be honest I wasn't surprised.

Alec Maxwell (Army)

We flew all types of aircraft off the *Implacable*—Sea Hornets (Mosquitos by any other name), Seafires, and even Blackburn Firebrands. They were dreadful aircraft, those Firebrands, probably the worst planes in the Fleet Air Arm.

Mind you, the Seafires were awkward beasts too. They were very delicate aircraft and tended to bounce over the side, particularly when they were being flown by RNVR pilots.

Flight decks were hazardous places. There were lots and lots of accidents, especially on landing. Several pilots and air crew got themselves killed while I was on board—and, as an aircraft handler, I had to help deal with the aftermath. None of it stopped the flying and we just had to continue with the planes and the personnel that we had been given.

George Moretta (Fleet Air Arm)

I was on the *Jutland*, a Battle-class destroyer. The Battle-class were big as far as destroyers were concerned and we used our ship's boats quite often. I was stoker on one of the motor boats. We were working with an Army Bomb Disposal Unit, dropping them off at Alderney in the Channel Islands. The soldiers were supposed to go down a scrambling net against the side of the ship while we lowered our boats.

A young seaman was working the falls—you were supposed to let go the after fall first, but he did it the wrong way round and the motor boat tipped, bow first, into the water.

I came up from the engine room of the motor boat when I felt her going. I could see what was about to happen and dived over the side as the motor boat hit the water and disintegrated. I kicked off my shoes and tried to get away from the side of the ship and the motor boat. It wasn't easy—swimming in your best gear was never easy and we were dressed up because of the 'combined ops' thing. All the 'big wigs', Army and Navy, were standing on the bridge watching the disaster.

It was freezing in that water and you had to keep swimming to keep the circulation going. When they finally launched another boat to pick up me and the rest of the motor boat crew the old *Jutland* was a good half a mile distant. When we finally got back on board they gave us a tot of rum to warm us all up. I was never too sure what happened to the rating who had caused the problem.

Stuart Ashdown (Navy)

The flight deck of an aircraft carrier is a pretty dangerous place. You need at least 30 knots of wind coming down the deck in order to give the aircraft the necessary lift. So it's always windy up there. Aircraft fly off into the wind and so we had to sail into the wind to facilitate this. When you're close to the edge of the deck it can be quite hairy.

I always found the rolling of the ship not too bad. But pitching, bows down and then up in the rollers, that was a different matter. Pitching certainly didn't help the pilots. They'd often lose the deck as they were coming in to land. Oh no, believe me, the flight deck of an aircraft carrier is certainly not for the faint hearted.

George Moretta (Fleet Air Arm)

Despite the danger and the problems, for many of the young national servicemen, life was still relatively enjoyable. They had few responsibilities and often viewed many of the challenges they were presented with as little more than a dare:

There were two huge stone pillars at the entrance to the Grand Harbour on Malta. We came in past them every time we made port. Somebody dared me to climb up and dive off one of them.

I ignored them the first few times, but eventually I couldn't resist the challenge. I climbed up and dived. It was a long way up and when I hit the water it was like hitting concrete from that height. I nearly broke my back.

We used to dive off the ship too. They'd pipe 'Hands to Bathe' when we were 2 or 3 miles off shore—shore? You couldn't see the shore we were that far out.

Anyway, in we'd go. The water was usually calm and clear. I'd swim down so I could see the bottom of the ship and sometimes go under her bows and come up on the other side. Then I'd creep along the side before going back and diving under again. The thought of danger or getting hurt never entered my mind.

Mind you, that wasn't always the case. There'd be guys on deck with rifles, keeping a look out for swordfish that used to come and jump around the hull of the ship. As soon as somebody yelled 'swordfish' you'd have thought we were practising for the Olympics.

Geoff Lewis (Navy)

I was out in Korea when peace was declared and was supposed to go up to the 38th Parallel where they were negotiating the release of prisoners. I was supposed to be recoding the details of men who'd been killed in action.

I can't say I was looking forward to it, particularly, although going up to the line that divided the two Koreas would have been interesting. But I'd been detailed for demob and when orders for the 38th Parallel came through I was already on the troop ship.

It's the weather conditions I remember most about Korea. You sweated all day, froze all night. Right next door to our camp was a rehabilitation centre—every one of the men in that camp was suffering from frostbite.

One piece of equipment everyone had was a poncho, supposedly to keep you dry. We used to use them as sleeping bags. But it was so cold at night that your sweat just froze on the inside.

Gordon Denley (Army)

Danger followed national servicemen right to the end of their time. Most of them had been counting off the days left to serve on their demob charts, but, even so, as the day of discharge drew nearer, there was an unbridled excitement in the air. That applied whether you had enjoyed your time in the armed forces or hated it:

My last couple of days in Cyprus went by in rather a blur. I could hardly sleep for excitement and I was right off my food. The only events I remember were that two Greeks were shot on the Saturday and a soldier drowned when he dived off a boat and hit his head on the bottom.

The 1st of May saw a 4.40 a.m. start, bus to Nicosia, customs, security, and then we were away—on a Hermes of Skyways of London. I was on the same flight as the Jimmy Edwards Show crowd, who had been entertaining and performing for the troops— Jimmy Edwards, Alec Finlay, etc. We had a very strong headwind and had to stop in Marseilles to refuel in addition to the normal stop in Malta.

We landed at London Airport just after midnight and went by BOAC bus to RAF Hendon. My last day in the RAF was 3 May.

Colin MacCallum (RAF)

For some of the men about to go home, away from conflict and danger, it was the pathos of places and situations that stayed with them:

> Just before we were due to be shipped out from Eritrea, a group of us, complete with bugles and part of a rifle company, went to the war cemetery at Keren. They blew the Last Post over the graves of the boys who had been killed in the country during the war. It was very moving.
>
> Years later, there was a letter in the *Daily Mail*, a man wanting information about that cemetery. An uncle of his had been killed in the Battle of Keren Gorge and was buried there. I wrote to the paper and asked if they'd pass on my letter. I was able to say that the man's uncle had had the Last Post sounded over his grave before the South Wales Borderers left the country. He could rest assured that his uncle had been given full honours.
>
> Henry Jones (Army)

The fear that something might happen to delay a posting out of a danger zone—a posting that, for many, was also a precursor to demob—was real and when that was backed up by the very real danger of terrorist activity it was just a question of holding your breath and praying.

11

Conscription:
How to Avoid It

National service was meant to be universal. However, there were a number of ways to avoid the call up, either by design or default. In the words of Peter Hennesey, 'piety and affliction could also keep you out of uniform.'[1] He was referring to the fact that exemptions from the call up were given to men who had mental health problems, who suffered from afflictions like TB, blindness, or physical disability, or who were clergymen.

In fact, the range of possible 'get outs' was a lot wider than that. Inevitably there were loopholes, as in all systems, but if men had the inclination there were numerous ways to avoid spending the customary two years in khaki or RAF blue. The government, taking semantics to a fine art, was clear that, apart from health and spiritual obligations, there was no such thing as an exemption. There was, however, a system of deferment:

> All men under the age of 26 are liable for National Service, but those in certain specified occupations are deferred for as long as they are employed in those particular occupations.[2]

The range of 'specified occupations' included a number of highly skilled scientists and engineers engaged on priority work for the government, shale oil underground workers, and a small number of police cadets. The key points were that the men had to remain in their alternative profession until the age of twenty-six and the work in question had to be essential to the good governance of the country.

Students at university were allowed to finish their course of studies and obtain their degrees before they were called up. There was no allowance for anyone taking higher degrees and deferment was only a temporary reprieve unless the student could somehow extend his period of study. However, as national service neared the end of its life, a course of studies at one of Britain's premier educational establishments often seemed like a good way to avoid the call up:

> I went to Swansea University in 1960, as soon as I finished school. I knew national service was coming to an end and while it had been spoken about during my adolescence—'It'll make a man of you' and sentiments like that—by 1960 it was clear the system would not last much longer.
>
> Robert Nisbet (Student)

I became eighteen in 1956, but when, a few weeks before that, I went to register for national service—as we all had to do—they turned me away as I was too young. 'Come back in a few weeks,' they told me. I wanted to become a solicitor and there were two ways to do that. I could spend three years at university or I could become articled and learn on the job. That took five years.

I would have happily gone and done my national service, but, with the delay, I thought, 'Hang it, I'll take articles.' And that was that. If I'd gone to register a few weeks later, my age would have been right and, before I knew it, I'd have been in the Army like everyone else. Fate, I suppose.

Keith Terry (Solicitor)

My rationale was to get my degree first and then see what happened after that. If I had to do national service that was fair enough, but I guessed it wouldn't happen. I can't say I was particularly worried about the call up, getting my degree was my main concern. As it happened, the last man was called up in 1960, the last man was discharged in 1963 and I got my degree in 1963. So the issue of doing or not doing my national service never arose after I went to Swansea University.

Robert Nisbet (Student)

I began work with a law firm in Dumfries Place in Cardiff in 1956. It was a practical course, really, studying in the evenings and at weekends and learning on the job, and it lasted until 1961. Although national service was still technically in place, they were no longer calling up young men. So the matter of joining up never surfaced again.

Keith Terry (Solicitor)

It was not just university students who could claim a deferment. Men who were on apprenticeships could also delay their call up until they had qualified. As with those studying for their degrees, however, it was only delaying the inevitable:

I went to school in Cheltenham, but left during the early years of the war to start training as a mechanic. After a while, I transferred to WARAG, working on tractors, combine harvesters, and the like. That meant I was in a reserved occupation as long as the war lasted. I tried to get into the Navy, but they wouldn't take me because of the reserved occupation thing. Once the war finished, I knew it was only a matter of time. By then I'd qualified as a mechanic and so I was called up in May 1946, at the end of wartime conscription and at the beginning of the peacetime call up.

Arthur Ainger (Army)

I managed to defer my call up until May 1957. I had an aircraft apprenticeship and that meant an automatic deferment until I'd finished my course. I kept finding more and more courses, more and more exams to study for—until, finally, I ran out of qualifications to take. That was it, the papers arrived and I was in the RAF.

Brian Chaplin (RAF)

When I was sixteen years old, I was given an engineering apprenticeship with Cammell Lairds and that qualified me for a deferment. At the age of eighteen I went for my national service medical, produced my indentures, and that was it, I heard no more.

After my apprenticeship, I went into the drawing office where I was working on the new *Ark Royal*. As long as you were working on vessels of national importance you could apply for a further deferment. And, no doubt about it, the *Ark Royal*, Britain's new aircraft carrier, was pretty important.

The chief draftsman came along one day and told me that people from the government were going to visit me regarding the deferment. 'They won't have a clue what you're doing,' he said. 'They just need to satisfy themselves that you're being genuine. Get all your drawings out and make sure the name *Ark Royal* can be seen at the top.'

Next day, these two guys in bowler hats came into the office. They asked a few questions and I answered. They glanced at the drawings and that was that. I was given a further two years deferment.

I worked there for the two years and then decided to go to sea. I was twenty-three years old and I became an engineer officer. I stayed at sea for the next three years.

Bob Campbell (Apprenticeship and Merchant Navy)

Bob Campbell went to sea when his period of deferment ran out. Occasionally, however, men decided to let their deferment slide and allow fate to take its course. Their reasons for this were many and varied:

I was eighteen years old when I was called up and in the middle of an apprenticeship at Cammell Lairds Shipyard. But I decided I'd had enough. Conditions in the yard were appalling, the smoke and stench and grime. Taken on their own that would have been bearable, but the way you were expected to live and work was dreadful.

The toilets, for example, well they were just a trough, little more than a hole in the ground. There was no canteen, nowhere to wash your hands, nowhere to sit and eat your sandwiches. The thought of enduring that for another two or three years was too much, so I gave up my exemption and joined the RAF.

Reg Gooding (RAF)

As opposed to studying at university or for a job, medical exemptions were not temporary. They were for life. The novelist and poet Herbert Williams contracted tuberculosis in May 1948 when he was just fifteen years old. His elder brother had been in and out of TB sanatoriums for several years and another brother, Bobby, had died of the disease earlier in the year. After being diagnosed with TB, Herbert spent two years in a sanatorium before being discharged in the winter of 1950:

> I'd not long come out of the sanatorium and was still recovering when the call up letter dropped through the letter box. I hadn't thought about national service, but now, suddenly, here they were, asking me to go for a medical.
>
> I went to see my doctor and he said it was a stupid notion as they'd never take me. But, he declared, I'd better go along to the medical. I was living in Aberystwyth and the medical board was in Swansea. It was a hell of a journey for a boy just out of TB hospital, winding country roads, narrow lanes, and so on.
>
> The doctors examined me and looked at my records. And they very quickly decided that the British Army could do without me. I was exempt from service. I'd gone all the way from Aberystwyth to Swansea for a ten-minute medical, the result of which was a foregone conclusion.

> Herbert Williams (Medical Exemption)

Herbert Williams knew what the result of his medical would be long before he turned up for examination, but for some young men medical exemption came as something of a surprise—and then only after considerable hardship:

> I'd been in the Army Cadets during the war—mainly to get something warm to wear! So afterwards, when national service came around, I didn't fancy all that marching again. I was about seventeen years old and a mate and I decided we'd stowaway on one of the ships in the docks. The *Gull Pool* it was, bound for Australia. We went up the gangplank and hid in one of the lifeboats.
>
> A couple of hours we lay there and then, suddenly, the tarpaulin was pulled back— the chief steward was putting in emergency supplies. After his initial surprise, he said, 'We aren't sailing until tonight. Come back later.' Off we went and came back that evening, just in time to see a young lad marching down the gangplank. He was carrying a suitcase and had obviously decided not to sail.
>
> We went to see the chief steward. There was only one job and he offered it to my mate. But when we went home to get his kit his father went ape—'Get up those stairs now. There's no way you're going to sea.' I went back to the ship, told the steward what had happened and got the berth.
>
> The ship sailed that night, with me on board, but there were troubles with her engines and she kept breaking down. In the end, they scrapped her and paid us all off. But it meant that I'd got my ticket as a merchant seaman. I sailed with the Merchant Navy for the next two years.

After two years, I thought it was time to come ashore—even though that meant doing my national service. I'd had enough of storms and cramped ships and rotten food. The Army couldn't possibly be as bad, I thought.

I went for my medical and to my amazement I was given Grade IV. They didn't want me! I'd had rheumatism as a child and it had affected my heart. They said I had a heart murmur! I was astounded—and a bit upset. I wouldn't have minded if I'd felt ill, but I was fighting fit. What really annoyed me was that I'd spent two years in the Merchant Navy and it wasn't necessary. I had a medical exemption all along.

James Morris (Medical Exemption)

As in wartime, the government soon decided that men could be exempted from military service if they were passed by a tribunal as conscientious objectors. Between 1945 and 1960, just over 9,000 people duly registered as objectors, most of them claiming exemption on grounds of religious and spiritual beliefs.[3]

Not all of these applications were successful and, faced by rejection, the applicant was either drafted into work as a stretcher bearer or, occasionally—when he refused to have anything to do with the armed forces—sent off to prison.

Strong political views often caused men to reject the call up. Several Scottish and Welsh Nationalists refused to serve in the British Army and, as a result, many of these found themselves in prison. The writer and Plaid Cymru supporter Meic Stephens had a lucky escape:

It took me five years to get a degree. There was one advantage to the fact that I'd taken so long to get letters after my name, which was that, in the meanwhile, military service had been abolished, fortunately for me, since I'd filled in some forms to the effect that I intended registering as a conscientious objector on political grounds but it wasn't necessary to go before a Tribunal after all. I heard nothing further from the authorities.

Meic Stephens (Plaid Cymru)
My Shoulder to the Wheel

Government work remained a sure way of avoiding the call up, right to the end. Scientists, engineers, and technical specialists were always needed, but, as with other loopholes, it did depend on the men staying in their posts until they reached the age of twenty-six:

My call up was deferred because I was working for the government. Firstly, I was at the firing ranges at Pendine in West Wales, quite close to Dylan Thomas's Boathouse. I was doing mechanical engineering, but the chief engineer wasn't impressed with the training my colleagues and I were being offered.

It resulted in four of us being transferred to the Royal Radar Establishment in Malvern. They had a self-contained college at Malvern, theory and practical on one complex. We stayed in the old County Hotel in Malvern, right in the centre of town. That was really good because we were in the middle of town, close to pubs and restaurants and the like.

I was at Malvern until 1957, specialising in instrument work. Then I had my medical for national service. I suppose I could have stayed on, doing government work, but I'd had enough. I wanted to do something else for a while and so I found myself in the RAF.

Gerry Evans (Mechanical Engineer)

After school in Porth, I took a chemistry degree at Cardiff. That was in 1950 and after getting my degree I was taken on by the Atomic Energy service. That meant, of course, that I was exempt from national service. They sent me to Dounreay up in Scotland.

I can't say I was very happy with the Atomic Energy set up in those days. There was a lot of high-level radioactivity in the storage tanks.

One of my friends—three of us were in school together, in university together, and went into Atomic Energy together—he was at Wincanton when there was a fire in the pile. The plant threw out a lot of radioactivity and there were real questions about its safety.

The plant at Dounreay never worked while I was there as we were part of the team sent up to commission it. But I left before it really got going.

I stayed with the Atomic Energy service until I was twenty-nine—not because I wanted to avoid national service, but because there was a job to do. After I left I went into teaching. Very different!

David Vivian Thomas (Atomic Energy Service)

My husband Roger was exempted from national service because he was working for Metropolitan Vickers on military radar. He was doing post-grad work and obviously it was considered of significant importance because they wanted to keep him. So he was given exemption and stayed with the company until 1961—by which time national service was coming to an end.

Vicky Smith (Wife of Electrical Engineer Roger)

Standing as a prospective member of parliament—provided you could find some party willing to adopt you as a candidate—was another way of avoiding the call up, particularly if you were successful and managed to get elected. To begin with, however, just the fact that you were running for election was enough to release you from military service (temporarily, at least). Several national servicemen put themselves up for election in the 1951 and 1955 elections, purely as a way of getting themselves out of the Army, even though they and the military authorities knew that they had little chance of being elected.

The government soon closed that particular loophole, although not entirely. Michael Heseltine somehow managed to gain permission to stand for election in 1959, in a seat he had no hope of winning. With national service clearly coming to the end of its days, he then ordered his solicitor to successfully argue that he did not need to return to the Army.[4]

One of the more unusual ways of avoiding conscription was to sign on as a regular. It was a tactic that was not as silly as it sounds. The pay as a regular serviceman was considerably better than the pittance received by those conscripted for national service and the prospects of promotion—which inevitably brought with it another increase in pay—were also much better. In an age when overseas travel was unusual, being a regular probably meant that at some time in your service you would more than likely spend one or two periods overseas:

> I joined the RAF in February 1959, initially for nine years but I extended it to 12. To begin with I wanted to fly, but my eyes weren't good enough and so I took an apprenticeship.
>
> I was promoted through the ranks, which wouldn't have happened if I'd been a national serviceman, from AC1 up to junior tech (which used, in those days, to be denoted by an upside down stripe) and, eventually, to sergeant. I knew my period of service was almost over so I never went higher than that.
>
> When I joined up, I knew that national service was coming to an end. But, amazingly, three or four months into my service I got a letter, telling me I was being called up. I wrote back saying I can't come. They queried that, of course, but the answer was simple—I'm already in!
>
> George Cheeseman (RAF Regular)

Regulars and national servicemen were mixed together in their billets and in the work environment. They often trained together (certainly for basic training) and by and large the two elements got on well enough:

> I had a great time with the national service boys. They were mates and work colleagues, no different from the rest of us. The RAF conscripts were, in the main, well-educated as the RAF had the pick, so I suppose that helped.
>
> Overseas postings? I was detailed to go to Woomera, the rocket-launching site in Australia. I was all prepared and even sold my car, a beautiful Singer Gazelle—and then the posting was cancelled. I was furious, no overseas posting and no car. Two weeks later, I was sent out to the Persian Gulf, an RAF base close to Dubai. There were only 100 blokes there. Apart from that it was all sand and camels.
>
> After six months they closed down the bases in Aden and hundreds of squaddies descended on us. It wasn't too bad, that posting. It was so hot you started at 7 a.m. and finished for the day by 1 p.m. I remember sitting in the open-air cinema and staring up at the flickering lights of satellites as they went over. I was there for twelve months before I came back to RAF Lynham in Wiltshire and, finally, St Athan in Wales—very different from the Persian Gulf.
>
> George Cheeseman (RAF Regular)

Sometimes men were given exemption for the strangest of reasons. Eleanor Morgan's father, Tom Davies, was granted his exemption because he was the only carpenter and joiner in the tiny West Wales village of Llandysul:

My father was the local wheelwright and being the only wood worker in the district he did lots of other jobs as well—one of them was making coffins. He was also the roofer for the village. There were few cars in those days and people relied on horse and cart, so a wheelwright was a very important person in a rural community like ours. The local people needed his skills and so he was exempted from the call up.

Eleanor Morgan (Daughter of Carpenter)

In the 1950s, coal was an essential fuel, both for the home and for industry. Coal mining had been crucial during the war, so much so that for the second half of the conflict one in every ten conscripts went to the mines—Bevin Boys played their part in winning the war. The same need to maintain the mining force at maximum levels of efficiency persisted once peace came in 1945.

If the dependency of the country on coal needed proving, it came during the dramatic winter of 1946–47, when power stations were shut, railway lines were blocked, and people in rural villages were cut off by the snow for weeks at a time. Small wonder, then, that coal mining was one of the jobs that qualified for exemption from military service.

Attracting men to work in the pits was not easy. Boys from the mining communities of Yorkshire, Northumberland, Wales, and the rest went to work underground because it was, sometimes, all they knew. They had seen their fathers go to the mines and their grandfathers before them—when their turn came they went into the pits, maybe not happily, but uncomplaining all the same. Yet mining was a dirty, dangerous, and draining profession and attracting new blood to the industry was not easy.

In reply to a question in parliament on 15 November 1951, when he was asked what steps the government was taking to attract more men into the coal mines, Sir Walter Monckton gave an unequivocal answer:

The alternative of entering or re-entering the coal-mining industry instead of the Armed Forces is being brought more prominently to the notice of young men registering for National Service.[5]

Despite government assurances, when faced by the option of two years in the Army or two years at the coal face, most young men happily plumped for the military. It was hardly surprising and yet those men who worked underground still retain a fondness for their former occupation. Bill Richards, now retired and writing books about his experiences, worked underground for many years:

I was a grammar school boy, but I never really applied myself to my studies and left in 1952. I was fifteen years old and after a few 'false starts' I went underground in January 1953. I started as a collier boy, but I was pretty soon made measuring clerk, measuring the output of coal as it came off the face. I had moved from 'men' to 'management'—and in those days there was a pretty clear divide between the two—on the other side of the fence.

It wasn't easy, usually because men had to share their earnings and someone who was clearing his ground in five days was effectively subsidising one who took seven. So there was a lot of ill feeling around and, inevitably, as the first line of management, a lot of it came my way. By the time I was seventeen and a half I'd had enough.

I knew I'd have to do my time in the armed forces, now I was no longer working underground. I thought I'd rather like the RAF uniform, the stories of the Battle of Britain and all that, and decided that I would try for the RAF when I went to register.

But when I went along to the Labour Exchange to let them know I was available for national service they told me I was too young and should come back in a few weeks. I had just over a month to wait and so I went back to work, underground. Six weeks, I told myself, I can do six weeks; six weeks and I'd be in the RAF.

I had nothing to lose, back in the old job. And I suppose I put my foot down with some of the more truculent miners. They were great blokes, but they needed a firm hand, as I now realised. Not brutal or unfair, just form and consistent.

Suddenly, the men and the management started to respect me—a difficult thing to manage. But I'd got over the worst and was enjoying life. 'I've cracked it,' I thought. 'I don't need the forces.'

And so I stayed in the mines, taking deferment and I can honestly say I never thought about national service again.

Bill Richards (Miner)

I worked in the mining industry, starting as an apprentice mine surveyor at the age of fifteen and carried on working underground until I was twenty-nine. Because I was underground—you had to be an underground worker, men on the surface didn't qualify—I was eligible for deferment and so national service never touched me.

More to the point, I can't say I even thought about it. That's the recklessness of youth, I suppose.

Howard Hawtin (Miner)

I'm glad now that there was that six-week delay when I went to register for national service. If I'd gone along at the right age, I'd have been in the RAF before you could blink.

I enjoyed my time in the mining industry—the second time, that is. There were so many characters there, superb men. I had, and still have, such a lot of respect for them. They worked for a pittance, cramming their bodies into spaces barely big enough to swing a sledge. Of course, not every one of them was a gem, but I spent fourteen years underground and although now I write and give talks about that time not one paragraph, not one book could ever capture the joy of my time underground.

Bill Richards (Miner)

If industry, usually in the form of coal mining, provided one way out of national service, agriculture was another. Britain had always imported much of its food from the colonies and from America, but the recent German U-boat campaign of the 1940s showed the foolishness of over-dependency on imported grain, wheat, and other foodstuffs. The country had been brought, virtually, to its knees twice by the submarine attacks of the First and Second World War and now the importance of maintaining a strong farming industry in Britain meant that men working in agriculture could also claim a deferment from their national service:

> My family moved to Lincolnshire when I was a teenager. When the time came to leave school, I needed a job and, in 1949, when I would have been eligible for national service, I was working on one of the local farms. And that meant—for the time being, at least—I was deferred as far as national service was concerned. I can't say I took up farm work to stay out of the forces, I just needed a job. Deferment was a by-product.
>
> The man we were working for paid piece-work. In other words, you didn't get a standard wage, you were paid for the amount of work you could do in a day and we were well paid. I was earning a lot more than I would have done in the Army, maybe £3 to £5 a week.
>
> There were over thirty people working on the farm, producing potatoes, sugar beet, wheat, and barley. We had Lincoln Red Cows and five tractors, which were used for various tasks around the farm. Having said that, we mainly used horses to pull the ploughs and there was a wide variety of horses still being used in the county—Suffolk Punches, Shires, Clydesdales. I loved working with the horses and spent most of my time with them.
>
> After two or three years, however, I became fed up with farm work. I couldn't see a future in it, certainly not with the horses. Sadly, as far as I was concerned, the future lay in tractors and I had no interest in them.
>
> The winter of 1951 was very wet and getting up at 6 a.m. and then taking an hour's cycle ride to work in the pouring rain wasn't much fun. The fields were just seas of mud. So I went to the recruiting office and even though I'd missed the call up I signed on with the Royal Marines as a regular. I spent the next twenty-two years in the Marines—it was certainly very different from my time on the farm.

> Don Hooley (Farm Worker)

Farm worker, miner, government employee, all of them virtually guaranteed exemption from military service, provided men stuck with their profession until the age of twenty-six. For some that was relatively easy, for others an impossibility. Whatever job men chose to do, not one of them came close to the surest and most consistent way of avoiding the call up—joining the Merchant Navy.

12

The Merchant Navy

Throughout the 1940s and '50s, Britain's Merchant Navy was the country's lifeline, freighters and tankers bringing goods into British ports and then taking exports out to foreign markets. In the immediate post-war years, ports and docks were still a hive of industry. Manning the merchant fleets was crucial, and was something that universal conscription could adversely affect. Small wonder then that merchant seamen were deferred from national service.

There were objections to the deferment of Merchant Navy sailors, however. In July 1955, Lord Glyn, at a sitting of the Lords, asked if the government would be prepared to order a review into the system that exempted waiters and stewards on board ship from national service. They were, in his opinion, not sailors in the true sense of the word. The response was immediate, a government spokesman declared:

> None of the large liners of the British Mercantile List would be able to sail were it not provided with a large number of catering staff without whom the lifeboats could not be manned.[1]

It appeared that waiters had to be proficient in boat handling as well as catering—it was not just liners. All ships needed stewards, men who in time of war became not just lifeboat handlers but gunners as well. The matter was duly dropped.

As with miners and government employees, the stipulation that men had to serve at sea until they were twenty-six also applied. Whether or not men deliberately chose to go to sea in the Merchant Navy remains a moot point:

> Joining the Merchant Navy as a way out of national service? I have no doubt that there were some who had that intention, but, from what I remember, one had to be twenty-six before one was exempted from the requirement to serve. It was really just a deferment until you reached that age and I believe that the vast majority of those who went to sea did so with a view to making it their career.

> Bryan Knights (Merchant Navy)

Engineer officers had to serve an apprenticeship with an engineering company before going to sea, while seamen and stewards often attended a pre-sea training school like the *Vindicatrix*. It was not compulsory, but deck officers also normally attended college before going to sea. That meant that many men would already be twenty or twenty-one before starting their careers, while, for the seamen, the starting age would have been about seventeen.

Even for ordinary deckhands, men who were qualified mainly by experience rather than formal study, the prospect of many years at sea stretched ahead of them like a jail sentence—unless they were very serious about choosing the sea as a career:

> It therefore meant that men would have to serve maybe ten years at sea to avoid national service, a long time to avoid a much lesser time as a serviceman.
>
> Bryan Knights (Merchant Navy)

Many ex-Merchant Navy sailors are adamant that nobody in their right mind would choose a life at sea rather than agree to a few brief years in the Army:

> You may find suggestions that some men joined the Merchant Navy to dodge the Army. Well, in my opinion, the only thing they were dodging was common sense. The forces got all their equipment and clothing supplied, hot or cold. In the Merchant Navy you had to get your own.
>
> Deckhand pay was not great so a lot of 'make do and mend' went on. Some sailors' idea of cold weather gear was to put their jersey on inside their shirt!
>
> Sleeping in sweltering steel boxes in the Red Sea, enduring force 10 or 11 storms in the North Atlantic in December, the possibility of being away from your family for years—on the other hand, conscription meant two years at Catterick or Aldershot, cricket and football every week, a camp cinema, and a monthly pass home to see your family. It was a stroll in the park—he says, tongue in cheek!
>
> Thomas Cullen (Merchant Navy)

As far as men choosing to serve in the Merchant Navy rather than the armed forces, well to be honest I'm a little bit sceptical. In my experience, there were a few, a very few, who took that option, but it was usually done by men from seafaring families. Or by those who were living in sea port areas.

> W. A. Sparks (Merchant Navy)

It is a valid viewpoint. For many youngsters, however, particularly those with a nautical background, joining the Merchant Navy instead of joining the Army or even the Royal Navy was a conscious decision. For many men, knowing that national service was on the horizon, life in the merchant marine was infinitely preferable to any of the armed forces:

My father was a Royal Navy man and I quite fancied the idea of going to sea, but in those days you'd have to have been born with a silver spoon in your mouth to get even a sniff of a commission. I'd been in the Air Cadets and hadn't really enjoyed that very much. All square bashing and no flying! National service, I thought, would have been more of the same.

So the Merchant Navy it was to be. Two or three of my friends, all of the same mind, joined Holts; I went to the Ellerman Line. That was April 1953. I joined as a cadet—some companies called us midshipmen, others apprentices—and after my four years indentures I was promoted to fourth officer. I went to Maritime College in Glasgow—now Strathclyde University—where they ran courses in subjects like naval architecture and navigation.

Bill Barker (Merchant Navy)

I served an apprenticeship in the RN Dockyard at Devonport and having seen the Navy from the inside, so to speak, I decided that service life wasn't for me. So I took a job with Alfred Holt and Co., the old Blue Funnel Line, as an electrician. And that, of course, exempted me from national service as long as I remained at sea until I reached the grand old age of twenty-six.

That must have been about 1958 and Holts were a pretty big and busy concern. In the days before container ships, we took general cargo on our outward trips, raw materials homeward. Living conditions, in the main, were good. At least on the ships I sailed on. Certainly they were much better than you'd find in the Army.

National service was hardly ever mentioned when we were sitting around, chatting, although it was clear that several of the younger blokes were in the Merchant Navy to avoid the call up. The older ones tended to be career men.

John Stroud (Merchant Navy)

It was always understood or arranged that I would go to sea, national service or not. My father founded General Engineering and Electric Welding on Swansea Docks, so sea faring and nautical things were in the blood. I went to sea in October 1952, a month before my seventeenth birthday. I was apprenticed to the Baron Line; that took four years, and then I spent another four years as a watch keeping officer.

I certainly didn't go to sea to avoid national service, but it was noticeable that a lot less people went to sea when the call up ended. It could have been coincidence; read what you like into that.

Roger Jones (Merchant Navy)

I trained as a seaman on the TS *Vindicatrix* at Sharpness. It was quite a hard regime on board and lots of lads didn't finish the course. They just disappeared or went AWOL in the night and you never saw them again. I'd always been interested in the sea and so I saw it through until I was eighteen. Then, like everyone, I went to register for national service.

They wanted me to sign for the Marines, but I wasn't too sure about that. I'd already been offered a berth with the Blue Funnel Line and when they asked me for my address I said, 'Somewhere at sea.' I don't think they were best pleased.

I spent eight years at sea. I went away as a deck boy and finished up as a quartermaster with the P&O Line.

Norman Bryce (Merchant Navy)

Bureaucracy was not always efficient as far as Merchant Navy sailors were concerned and sometimes the families of men who were away at sea had to cope with the worry and concern those mindless errors created:

I was indentured as an engineering apprentice with the Admiralty at the Naval Dockyard, Rosyth. I finished this in August 1948 and joined the Merchant Navy three months later. I was with the Clan Line most of the time, making voyages to South Africa, Sri Lanka, and what is now Bangladesh.

During one of these voyages, sometime in 1949, a letter was sent to my home address saying that I was being called up and adding that anybody who ignored such a summons was liable to be arrested. My mother was very concerned and told the Ministry of Labour that I was at sea, but would report to them on my return.

When I got back home, I reported to the Ministry of Labour Office in Edinburgh and was given a formal interview. When they saw that I was in the Merchant Navy and was, like all the staff of the Clan Line, on a two-year contract—and, importantly, hadn't joined the MN just to escape national service—they were quite understanding.

David H. Sellars (Clan Line: Merchant Navy)

In an attempt to prevent any further misunderstanding or any future problems, David Sellars was issued with a registration card:

They gave me a registration card and told me that I was to carry it with me at all times. In particular, I had to carry it when I was ashore, on leave. If the civil or military police happened to stop me and ask why I wasn't in the forces I had to show the card and explain that I was in the Merchant Navy.

David H. Sellars (Clan Line: Merchant Navy)

While men who joined the Merchant Navy were guaranteed to see the world, conditions on board ship were not easy, particularly on the tramp steamers that were in the last vestiges of their life, trading around the globe and picking up cargoes wherever they could. However, there were compensations:

My first ship was the *British Advocate*, a tanker run by the British Tanker Company. I didn't do pre-sea training. A lot of the deck officers did—engineering officers had to— probably about 60 per cent of them attending one or other of the training schools and ships around the country. Me, I remember sitting at Pwllcrochan on Milford Haven one day and seeing this RFA tanker coming in. I remember thinking that might be a good job, applied to the company and was taken on.

It was a case, as an apprentice, of learning on the job. The *British Advocate* was really just like a tramp steamer. We had no real pattern to our trips, we just went all over the place picking up cargoes of crude oil and bringing them back.

It meant, of course, that I saw some amazing places. We were in Tripoli and Lebanon quite often. I saw lots of Africa and India, mostly the coastal areas. But I was also in Burma, Malaya, Australia, Japan, and Hong Kong. Strangely, I never went to the USA or Canada.

Ken MacCallum (Deck Officer: Merchant Navy)

My first trip was taking pontoons out to the Army in Korea, so that the soldiers could build bridges across ravines and rivers. We didn't go all the way to Korea, but dropped off our cargo at Kuri in Japan. It was quite close to Hiroshima where the first atom bomb had been dropped in 1945. It certainly gave you a weird sort of feeling, being that close to such a major bomb site. We were at Kuri when the Korean ceasefire was signed.

After that I went all over the world, the Far East, Jamaica, the Philippines. I went through the Panama Canal four times. That was a beautiful transit. It used to take a couple of days, lots of locks to get through. When you went through the Suez Canal you were through in a day—unless you got held up in the Bitter lakes to allow a north bound convoy to come through.

I can't say I was ever particularly impressed by the Suez Canal. It was a bit like sailing down a ditch, I always thought. The Panama Canal, in contrast, was very scenic—and very narrow in parts. It's actually a north-south canal, not east-west, like most people think. All the locks had 'mules', locomotives on a track alongside the canal, to keep you in the centre. It was quite an experience, each time you went through.

Bill Barker (Merchant Navy)

Life in the Merchant Navy in the 1940s and '50s—in what were, had they known it, the dying days of the British maritime industry—was certainly not easy. Hours were long, wages were low, conditions were desperate, and ships were out of date. Yet, there was no money to build new vessels and make improvements. Sailors just had to make do with what they had:

If you didn't like life at sea, the Merchant Navy was no bed of roses. It wasn't long after the end of the war and some of the shipping companies could be very difficult. I know that if I hadn't liked the life I'd have left, national service or not. As it happened I loved being at sea, despite the appalling food and the damp conditions. I served from 1951 until 1960 and only left after I'd got married and my first son was born. If it hadn't been for that I'd have stayed on.

Of course it was difficult. My first ship, the *Thistlemuir*, had just come back from Korea where she'd been delivering tanks to the troops. I had to share a cabin with three others. She was a steam vessel and she was infested with cockroaches; they loved steam and the hot, humid conditions. They were everywhere, thousands of the things.

It was dangerous, too. For three years we ran supplies to Cyprus during the EOKA emergency. Explosives, munitions, supplies, we carried it all for the British troops. All the times I was in Famagusta I never went more than a few hundred yards away from the dock. Famagusta was deep in the Turkish part of Cyprus, so I suppose we were reasonably safe. But not totally.

One of the company ships had a small explosive device attached under the gangway. It blew a hole in the side of the ship. Luckily nobody was injured, but it just showed nobody was safe out there, no matter what precautions you took.

Thomas Cullen (Deck Officer: Merchant Navy)

In 1954, they flew me to Vancouver as an EDH. I loved the city, but, unfortunately, I fell down a deck hold of the ship. Some clown had left the hatch cover off and when I stepped onto the tarpaulin I just went straight through. I broke all my teeth and ended up in hospital.

On our way to Hamburg once, we hit an acoustic mine, a relic of the war. It must have been bobbing about for years. There had been so many dropped, British and German, that it was impossible to pick them all up after the war. Anyway, we hit this mine and the thing exploded. The ship wasn't too badly damaged, but I got hit in the face by part of the radio. Danger everywhere!

Norman Bryce (Merchant Navy)

As an apprentice you were never left in sole charge of the bridge. The watch keeping officers and the Old Man just wouldn't take the risk. Apart from Christmas Day, when they chucked you up there and headed off to enjoy lunch and a drink—always with the advice: 'And make sure you don't bloody hit anything!'

Ken MacCallum (Merchant Navy)

I was a cadet on the *Worcester* training ship from 1948 to 1950. She was moored on the Thames, one of two officer training ships—the other was the *Conway* up on the Menai Straits.

As a cadet RNR, I'd have gone directly to the Royal Navy if war had ever broken out. As it was, I joined Ellermans as an apprentice before getting promoted to third mate, second mate, and so on. I finished up as the master of a sand dredger operating out of Bristol.

Several of the boys in the Merchant Navy—at least when I was at sea—became pretty fed up with conditions, the old ships and poor food, and just gave it up. They knew they'd have to do national service, but they obviously thought it was an acceptable alternative to the hard life at sea.

Terry Lyons (Merchant Navy)

Harsh living conditions and dangerous moments were, for most sailors, just part of the job. They were sometimes compensated for by beautiful scenery and exotic destinations—sometimes, but not always. The habits and behaviour of some of the people they sailed with were also an occasional cause for concern:

Some of those shipping companies were pretty tight-fisted. They wanted extra work out of you, but they wouldn't pay for it. We used to say things like 'never join the Bank Line, they'll just starve you'. There was an element of truth in our comments.

When I joined the *Thistlemuir*, I was just a boy, but I had to travel right across the country from Liverpool to Immingham Docks. It felt like I was going to another world.

Our chief steward—and the second steward as well, come to that—they had been at sea during the war and were both still 'torpedo happy'. Every bang, every lurch of the ship, they were all over the place.

When you'd call the chief in the morning, he'd shoot up in his bed, straight as a die. If your head was in the way you could be easily knocked out. You learned, quickly, to stand in the cabin door when you called him.

Thomas Cullen (Merchant Navy)

Looking back now there were, obviously, some hairy moments, but, at the time you didn't really notice things like rough weather, storms, or gales. It was just part of the job.

We were off Port Said during the Egyptian crisis. The US 7th Fleet was there as well and this destroyer came charging up, swung round parallel to us and began signalling. 'What cargo are you carrying?' Our reply was simply 'general'.

It obviously didn't please him because three times he made the same request. He obviously wanted more details. I got Sparks up to answer his questions—in detail. He had no right to ask, but he had guns and they were trained on us.

Ken MacCallum (Merchant Navy)

The jobs that Merchant Navy sailors undertook were many and varied. The phrase 'going to sea' covered a multitude of sins, and joining the Merchant Navy could see young men working on fishing boats in the North Sea or on general cargo vessels trading around the world, on luxurious passenger liners in the Caribbean or on massive oil tankers headed for the Persian Gulf:

When my call up age came, I was already in the Merchant Navy. As an eighteen year old, I was third radio officer in the *New Australia*, taking thousands of £10 immigrants—the Ten Pound Poms as they were called—out to start a new life in Australia. I served in several different ships, working for the Marconi Company, and stayed at sea until I was twenty-five. Then I went to work for the BBC before immigrating to New Zealand.

Mike Hartson (Radio Operator: Merchant Navy)

I did my apprenticeship in engineering, qualifying in October 1953. And then I had a decision to make—national service or the Merchant Navy. It was no choice, really, as companies like Cunard or Union Castle were paying around about £40 a month—a hell of a lot more than you'd get in the Army or Navy.

Twenty-seven of us qualified at the same time. I was one of five who joined Cunard, in my case as an engineer. My first ship was the old *Queen Elizabeth*. After a while, I was transferred to the *Queen Mary* and we were involved in regular trans-Atlantic runs, from Southampton to Cherbourg to pick up French passengers then across to New York.

It took us about four hours to get full steam up and then we just ploughed along. The first-class passengers had a luxurious time on board, but the third-class cabins were down next to the boiler rooms. Conditions there were very basic and the cabins got very hot.

As an officer I was well treated by Cunard. My cabin was a single one, on the sun deck. We had a Mess Room, but we dined off the first-class menu, complete with waiter service. There was a steward who served about twelve of the Officer Cabins. We also had a lounge—but no bar. We had to order drinks through the cabin steward and we had to pay for them. Having said that, it was duty free and we were entitled to one bottle of spirits per trip.

It was a good life. In summer we only stayed in New York for twenty-four hours, but in winter we were there for two or three days. You could get off ship, go to Coney Island, or see a show on Broadway. The engineering department even took on the caterers at cricket. We caught the ferry across to Staten Island and played there. Yes, all in all, a good time.

Brian Walters (Cunard Line: Merchant Navy)

I was doing an apprenticeship as a shipwright at Vickers Armstrong, due to finish in 1956. Then I heard that you could do the last six months of your apprenticeship at sea. I got clearance from the personnel department and within weeks I was at sea with the Elder Demster Line, on board the *Accra*, a motor vessel that they ran.

We went down the African coast to Lagos, but on the way back I went down with appendicitis. Luckily, I managed to get home before it 'exploded'. When I'd recuperated I joined the Orient Line and made three trips on the RMS *Orontes* as chief carpenter.

I enjoyed my time at sea, but I make no bones about it—I joined the Merchant Navy rather than go into the forces. After the *Orontes*, I served in lots of different ships, including the Orient Line's first tanker, the *Garonne*. But I was working for the Port Line when I reached the age of twenty-six and when they said I was due to go out to Australia and New Zealand again, I came ashore. That trip would have lasted four or five months and I'd recently got married. Neither my wife nor me fancied that length of separation.

Gordon Burrow (Carpenter: Merchant Navy)

Most of my time with Canadian Pacific, I was working on the trans-Atlantic route from Liverpool to Quebec and Montreal. It was great in the summer but there were some tremendous storms in winter. The Bay of Fundy was particularly bad.

It was a six-day crossing and in winter, in our cabins up on the boat deck, we were freezing. Still, I suppose a Nissen hut would have been worse. I always used to say that we were just a ferry boat service across the Atlantic, albeit a very luxurious one.

Then, at the end of 1957, they put us on cruising. We sailed out of New York on the *Empress of England*, a month cruise at a time, taking American tourists down to the Caribbean. It was wonderful because the ship only moved at night, and then slowly so as not to disturb the passengers. By the time they'd woken up, we had arrived at the next island and spent the day at anchor.

The captain always had a car provided for him at each port. After a while he got fed up using it and anyone who fancied a trip could jump in and away. I remember driving alongside the Panama Canal and going all the way around Jamaica. And I was being paid for it.'

Bob Campbell (Engineer Officer: Canadian Pacific)

I served my time as an electrician with Campbell and Isherwoods in Cardiff Docks and was deferred, while I completed my training. Being in the docks, I was used to ships and sailors and had a hankering for a bit of adventure. I went to sea in 1951 as a junior engineer for Elders and Fifes before moving on to tankers. Over the next few years I went all over the place, from the Caribbean to the Baltic.

Italy was one of the most interesting places—at Bari we had to discharge our cargo by lighter before going alongside. It was all to do with wrecks from the war, there were so many of them, all over the place.

I ended up as second electrician on the *Pretoria Castle*, part of the Union Castle Line. Our regular run was leaving Southampton at 4 p.m. on a Thursday, maybe stopping at Madeira, but finishing up at Cape Town. Then back to Southampton, two weeks for every trip.

Howard McFadden (Electrician: Merchant Navy)

One thing sailors the world over could be totally sure about was that life was never simple. Mistakes, problems, accidents, and complications beset everyone who ever went to sea—or didn't, as the case may be:

In the late '50s, when I went to sea, Holt's had more electricians and junior engineers than they needed. But they did need extra hands to carry out repairs and to service equipment when ships were in port.

I clearly remember that in Liverpool there was a group of lads who never went to sea at all, yet they were still regarded as Merchant Seamen. There was never, as far as I know, any sort of check on how often a man was at sea or anything like that. As long as they had their discharge book and a Merchant Navy ID card that was all they needed. I know I had periods ashore, in between trips or ships, and nobody ever checked on me.

John Stroud (Engineer: Holts Line)

Perhaps John Stroud was lucky. Certainly other men in the Merchant Navy have a different recollection of officialdom:

When I went to sea I reckoned the national service people had forgotten all about me. Not a chance.

I came ashore after one trip and was relaxing, having a holiday you might say. Suddenly there was a letter—if you don't get back to sea pronto we'll clobber you for the forces. I didn't fancy the Army and I loved being at sea. So I signed on again pretty quickly. I still don't know how they worked out I'd come ashore. After all, it was only for a few weeks.

Howard McFadden (Electrician: Merchant Navy)

Sailors, they say, have girls in every port. Whether that is just a cliché, a legend, or is really true is another matter. However, for some people, romance certainly bloomed and blossomed while they were serving in the Merchant Navy:

Gordon and I met while we were working on board ship. It was on the *Orontes* where he was the chief carpenter and I was a children's stewardess. That was in 1957. When we became involved and then married, I left the sea and set up home in Gravesend. He kept on working on the ships for a couple more years.

It wasn't easy, him being away for long periods, but you got used to it. I was working so I always had something to do, to keep my mind busy. What really annoyed me were banks or companies that wanted my husband's signature. They wouldn't accept mine because I was just a woman! I ask you. It was so stupid—not to mention sexist. There was no way I could get Gordon's for them as he was away at sea, at least not until he came home on leave. Thank God things are different now.

Anne Burrow (Wife of sailor)

The Merchant Navy offered an alternative to two years of national service. Opinion is divided as to whether men took that option in an attempt to avoid square bashing or whether they wanted to carve out careers for themselves at sea. Either way, it provides an interesting addendum to the national service experience.

13

The Girls They Left Behind Them

National service undoubtedly caused great disruption in people's lives. Men had to put their careers on hold, businesses were often thrown into disarray, and the loss to the economy as young men who would otherwise have been making a significant contribution to society was enormous.

There was also the little matter of personal relationships that were put under immense strain by enforced partings that sometimes lasted for many months. For the women who were left behind when their menfolk went off for their two years' service, there is no doubt that they suffered considerable degrees of hardship and discomfort. Little thought was ever given to the situation of wives and girlfriends. Most of the new recruits would have been just eighteen years of age and, in the minds of those in government, such men would not have been engaged or involved in serious relationships. Certainly very few of them would have been married—or so the 'powers that be' thought. Such an attitude was presumptuous and took next to no account of individual feelings and situations.

There was also the problem of men who deferred their service, either by taking an apprenticeship or by going to university. Such people would have been considerably older when they were finally called up and they, almost certainly, would have been involved in serious relationships with members of the opposite sex. Many of them would have got themselves engaged or, in more cases than were ever imagined by government ministers and the high command, were married with children to care for.

Even if they were not married, late adolescence had always been a time to fall in love. It was—and is—a period in the lives of youngsters when feelings are heightened and it seems as if nothing else matters but expressing those feelings for the recipient of your love. Such emotions were bound to cloud issues and make an enforced separation doubly painful.

Colin MacCallum was considering applying for a deferment when he left school in June 1953. He wanted to begin a career in accountancy and was heavily into the problem of applications and deferment interviews:

To complicate things, I fell in love for the first time. I was nearly eighteen and the object of my affections was the girl around the corner—a lively, attractive, golden-haired girl whom I had known since I was about eight years old. Hours were spent walking with her all around the neighbourhood and having tea at her place. My world was upside down.

Colin MacCallum (RAF)

When his application for deferment was turned down, Colin MacCallum found himself heading for a two-year stint in the RAF. His concerns and worries over his girlfriend, however, had not gone away. If anything, with typical teenage angst, they had increased:

Another worry at this time—and this time it was really serious—was that my girlfriend was almost a year older than me and I was worried that this would cause a problem 'later'. My Mum reassured me that it wouldn't matter. She was eight months older than my dad and she reminded me that my girlfriend's granny was a year older than her grandpa and they had been married for fifty years. I felt much better after that.

Colin MacCallum (RAF)

Heartache and worry about things like bromide in the tea could not stop any of the recruits thinking about that wonderful period when basic training would be over and they would be entitled to a brief period of leave before the next part of their ordeal:

The train didn't get to Glasgow until 9.16 p.m., but my sweetheart was waiting on the platform. And so was my dad. She had met him, wandering along outside the station. He was going to 'have a look at the trains'. 'The four-day leave vanished in a welter of long walks with my girlfriend and with my dad and siblings. There were teas and lunches at her house and at ours. It was great to wear fine flannels and a sports jacket again. We even found time to go and see *The Moon Is Blue* with David Niven, David Holden, and Maggie McNamara. A week after I got back, I got a letter from my girlfriend hoping I was drinking lots of tea and staying away from Walsall and Cannock.

Colin MacCallum (RAF)

Misery, heartache, and longing for the whole business to be over were not just the preserve of the soldiers and airmen. Wives and girlfriends knew what their loved ones were going through and they, like the men themselves, were powerless to do anything about it:

I wasn't involved with Ian when he did his national service. I knew him, of course— well, we lived in a very rural part of Scotland and he was one of the boys we hung around with. But by the time he went back to do his reserve training we were courting.

I know it was only two weeks, but I hated it. I missed him. I don't know how I'd have got on if we'd been together when he was in the RAF Regiment and away for two years.

Ruth Norrie (wife of Ian Norrie, RAF Regiment)

Charles and I weren't married when he was called up, but we were engaged. I can't say I liked him being away, but when he finished basic training he told me that he'd been posted to Bristol. That was quite close and I was really happy. Then he came home on leave and told me the posting had been changed. He was going to Cyprus. I was devastated.

We both knew that national service was something that had to be done and so, in a way, we didn't mind. But Cyprus then was in the throes of the EOAKA terrorist campaign and it was dangerous. He and his mates, they weren't allowed out because there were shootings and bombings all the time—at least until his last few months over there.

To make matters worse, he volunteered to ride shotgun on the wagons, sitting on the bonnet with his rifle. He was just bored because with the emergency and everything he couldn't go anywhere or do anything. So it was, really, just something to do.

I think it was just as well I didn't know anything about that until he was demobbed. He couldn't write to me about it because all the letters were censored. Thank goodness, I say.

Joan Blake (wife of Charles Roy Blake, RAF)

Tony was called up in the summer of 1960 and we got married in the October. They gave him a short bit of leave—not long, just a few days, long enough to get married, but not long enough for a honeymoon.

I lived with my mother in the Canton area of Cardiff so I had company. Even so I was very upset to start with. I missed him and hated it all. But you get used to it. I suppose you can get used to everything if you're given long enough.

Joan McCarthy (wife of Tony McCarthy, Army)

It was hard, emotionally. We both knew that Len would have to do his period of national service even though, even in the late 1950s, people were talking about the system ending. So when the call-up papers arrived there was a lurch of the heart, but there was that feeling of 'well, it's come at last'. At least it stopped the uncertainty.

Judith Skipper (wife of Len Skipper, Army)

Communication in the 1940s and '50s was not easy. Very few people had telephones and the concept of a mobile phone was still, really, a piece of science fiction. The only way soldiers, sailors, and airmen had of contacting their loved ones was by letter. Sometimes the Army and all of the services seemed to be full of people who simply did not care:

> We used to write once or twice a week, but he was limited what he could say because all the letters were censored. It made you very self-conscious, knowing that someone else would be reading your letters before you or him.

Joan Blake

> There was a real cock-up over my leave when my baby was born. I'd been married all my time in the Army, but then my wife became pregnant. I arranged to have leave when she was due to give birth, but the major in charge either forgot or didn't bother to log it. So I was stuck in Amsterdam and she had to cope with all that on her own. It wasn't easy for her and I was damned angry, but there was nothing we could do about it. It meant that I missed the first few months of my baby's life.

Brian Collins (Army)

Sometimes it was more than just a few months that soldiers missed. It was, perhaps, not as traumatic as the Second World War, when men were sometimes away from newly born children for years on end, but this was peacetime and the lack of compassion shown by many of those in charge rankled with national servicemen:

> We were living with Len's mother in Hillingdon when he was called up. His father had died not long before and it was a way of helping her through the grief. Then Len was called up and was posted to Hong Kong. Our son Kevin had been born a few months before and this, along with the recent death of his father made us hope that he could get a compassionate posting close to home. He explained it all to the officers, but it was no use and he ended up on a troop ship out to Hong Kong.
>
> I didn't see him all the time he was out there. We wrote, of course, but it wasn't the same. And of course it meant that he missed the first few years of Kevin's life, missed all those milestones like learning to walk and talk. Kevin didn't know his dad when Len finally came home—all he'd seen of him up to then were photographs.

Judith Skipper

> You couldn't question decisions that had been made, even though they were about you and your family. You made your requests and then got on with the job. I suppose, in those days, you just didn't question authority. I can't see people these days putting up with it.

Len Skipper (Army)

Support mechanisms from the services were virtually non-existent. If men were lucky, they would receive a little leave when there were problems at home, but this was not universal. A lot depended on the attitude of those in charge and, if the man was posted close enough to his home, there was always the possibility of a little extra contact:

> Tony was doing training at Brecon and that wasn't too far from Cardiff. One of our neighbours had a car—the only one in the street—and he used to drive me, over the Beacons to Brecon.
>
> After Tony had finished for the day, he'd get a pass and come out to meet me. We went to the pictures or we sat in a café with his mates. It wasn't a lot of contact, but it was better than nothing. Of course, all that finished when they posted him to Germany.

Joan McCarthy

> While Charles was in Cyprus his grandmother died. He asked for compassionate leave, but it was turned down—whether that was because of the EOKA emergency or not I don't know. That was hard for all of us.

Joan Blake

> Support from the Army? It didn't happen. I lived with my mother and the Army sent me an allowance every month—I suppose that was taken out of Tony's pay.
>
> He used to get leave, usually quite short periods, though, once, he got bitten by a horsefly while he was standing on the station in Germany, waiting to come home. By the time he got to Cardiff, his foot was swollen up like a balloon. He couldn't get his boots on. The doctor signed him off and he was home for about a month.
>
> They were very hard, the Army. Our first Christmas—the first Christmas of our married life—he was away and couldn't get leave. So I worked Christmas Day in the telephone exchange—it was better than sitting at home, moping.

Joan McCarthy

> I used to get an allowance from the Army. I can't remember how much, somewhere in the region of £5 I think. I remember going to the post office to collect it. They adjusted the amount occasionally, added a few pence or shillings but it was never very much.
>
> My support mechanism came from my family. I had seven sisters and I'd visit as often as I could. We all had young children and, I suppose, that more or less kept us going.

Judith Skipper

Many national servicemen quickly decided that permanent relationships could wait until they were demobbed. However, it did not stop them actively seeking out female company whenever they had a few moments of leisure:

> When I was doing my officer training on the Isle of Man, I had a little scooter. It meant that I could get into Douglas in the evenings and look for girls. At the Majestic Hotel in the town each table had a telephone and that meant you could ring up a girl on the other side of the room, ask her for a date, whatever.
>
> In town one evening, I saw this amazing-looking girl. We chatted and it transpired that she was the daughter of the leader of the council on the island. That was a very useful contact—it meant that the training certainly wasn't wasted.

Brian Chaplin (RAF)

> I eventually married a girl who was the daughter of an RSM. I'd known her before I went into the Army, but we quarrelled. I told her I'd been called up and she laughed—'Serve you right,' she said. When I came out of the Army, we decided to get married and, as you did in those days, I went to ask her father for permission to wed his daughter. 'What's she worth?' he asked.
>
> 'Ten Woodbines?'
>
> 'Done.'

Arthur Ainger (Army)

When demob happened, most of the girls or women who had sat at home and waited felt instant relief. Their period of purgatory was over:

> It was hard for Charles and me. He had finished his apprenticeship on the Friday and was in the RAF on the following Monday. All the time he was in Cyprus, he was living under canvas so conditions weren't good.
>
> But he came out and we were married six months later. They'd asked him to stay on, but he said no. He'd had enough—and so had I.

Joan Blake

> I was so happy to have Len back. It was as if life—his and mine—was on hold while he was in the Army and now we could pick up the pieces and start again.

Judith Skipper

Tony was serving with the South Wales Borderers in Germany, with the BAOR. Because they suddenly built the Berlin Wall, his two-year enlistment was extended by another six months. John Profumo was the minister concerned, the man who added those extra few months—he wasn't a popular man at that moment in time, I can tell you.

In the end, Tony only did an extra four months because I had a baby in September 1962 and they let him out early. He must have been one of the last national servicemen.

Joan McCarthy

Sadly, not all of the friendships and relationships between servicemen and their wives and girlfriends ended happily. It was, perhaps, inevitable:

I never married my sweetheart. Amid floods of mutual tears, I broke off our unofficial engagement shortly after I started a four-year degree course. We had been going together for more than five years, two of which were at long distance while I was in the RAF. During that time, we wrote to each other almost every day, thousands of words, hundreds of letters, millions of sighs, and many a warm glow. I'm sure this relationship kept me out of trouble and we parted, both still virgins! How times have changed.

Colin MacCallum (RAF)

Nobody denies the harshness of national service as far as the men were concerned. The concerns and problems of the women in their lives have never really been explored.

14

Demob

In a survey conducted by the Army and published in Brassey's *Annual* for 1956, it was reported that, while 10 per cent of servicemen hated life in the armed forces, 15 per cent loved it and the rest—some 75 per cent of all conscripts—accepted service life, but longed for the day when it would finally be over and they could return to Civvie Street.[1]

The percentages are not surprising. National service was an imposition and, no matter how much men had enjoyed their time in the Army, Navy, or RAF, the desire to return to normality was strong and vibrant. As the day for demob grew gradually, but inexorably closer, nobody could ever say that he was truly sorry the experience was almost over. Yet most men about to be demobbed would admit to mixed-feelings. They had made friends and experienced things they might never have otherwise thought about. They had developed skills and they had often pushed themselves to levels of achievement that were quite remarkable. However they felt about their period of national service, one thing was clear—they would never be the same again.

Many conscripts kept demob charts, calendars where they would mark off the days they had left to serve. They knew when their turn was approaching and, as a consequence, demob parties were always being held in every military camp, both in Britain and abroad:

We called it demob night. Whenever somebody was leaving, finishing their time, there'd be a party, some sort of celebration. It wasn't anything special, just a group of mates coming together for a few drinks and maybe a singsong, to wish the bloke who was going all the best. I think I must have attended dozens of them. In a way, they were quite sad because, no matter how much you promised to keep in touch, deep down we all knew that the chances of seeing the bloke again were very slim.

Alun Williams (RAF)

There were always parties, demob parties, to mark someone leaving and going home. Sometimes it seemed they happened every week. To start with, when you first went in, they were a bit depressing—the bloke was leaving, but your time had only just begun.

Then, the longer you served and the closer your own demob got, the more excited you became and the more interesting the parties were—'my turn soon', that type of thing.

George Best (RAF)

The actual process of demob varied for everyone. For most men, it was a case of returning to their base or depot, handing in equipment and clothes, and getting signed off. After that, they were free to leave the camp and head home.

Unlike soldiers who had served in the Second World War, there were no demob suits, with spivs waiting to buy them as soon as men came out of the door. Instead, there was just the notification of a bit of paid demob leave and then back to your family and friends. Reactions to this depended on the person:

I was demobbed in 1963, one of the last national servicemen to be discharged. I would have liked to sign on permanently, but with a wife and new baby it wasn't appropriate. When demob day came around, because I was one of the last national servicemen, they stuck me in a Champ, a jeep, and drove me round and round the camp. People were out cheering and shouting, waving and jumping about. It was a really good send off.

Brian Wheeler (Army)

I started my national service in March 1959, which was quite late in the call-up process. Because of that, because they really did not want to be bothered with us, I think, I only did twenty-two months, not the customary twenty-four—surplus to requirements, you might say. I was asked to sign on full time; my engineer officer really wanted me to stay, but I'd had enough. Even though I'd enjoyed my time in the Navy, I wanted out.

I was on HMS *Jutland*, out in the Med when my time for release came and they flew me home in an RAF Hastings. I went back to Plymouth, to HMS *Raleigh*. And although I hadn't seen them since basic training, I met up with most of the guys I'd trained with. I hadn't seen them for nearly two years and now we were all getting discharged at the same time.

Stuart Ashdown (Navy)

I was demobbed in August 1958. I swore I'd never wear another uniform in my life, but I had no job to go to and my father suggested I try the police—after all, that's what I'd been doing in the Rock Apes. I did try working as a fireman, but it wasn't for me and so I took dad's advice. I went along to the police station, filled in an application form, and by October 1958 I was in. I served as a policeman for nearly thirty years.

John Williams (RAF Regiment)

As demob approached, I did seriously think about staying on in the Navy. After two years, I was quite a contented sailor. But it was 1950 and during my time in the service nearly all the sailors were wartime men who'd been in a lot longer than me. There was very little chance of promotion and I decided I had better opportunities in Civvie Street.

George Moretta (Fleet Air Arm)

There was a real sense of loss for some men, a strange nostalgic emotion that was hard to place as they took their final farewells to the armed forces. Two years earlier, they would have laughed aloud at such feelings, but now, after all their experiences, many of them had to admit that, no matter how much they wanted to be home, they would miss their comrades and their units:

I wasn't desperate to get out of the Navy—looking back now, I'd say those two years were some of the best years of my life. I was young, fit, and single and the experiences, well, they were unreal for a boy from Aberavon in South Wales. After two years, I was into the life style, enjoying the good times, putting up with the bad.

It's hard to put into words, but there was a real sense of anti-climax when demob came around. Something was ending, a part of my life, and I wasn't sure what to feel. I remember pacing out the full length of the *Cumberland*, my ship, bow to stern, trying to remember it all I suppose. I tell you what, she was a massive ship. I went onto the *Ark Royal*, just to look around and I really felt that the *Cumberland* was bigger.

Geoff Lewis (Navy)

I was due for demob on 28 March 1953, but there was a football match and so I stayed on to play in that and left the next day. I'd never have believed that possible when I first went in. Times change, I suppose.

Next day, I took my forms around and got them signed, then I walked to the bus stop. I sat there with my little case, miles away, waiting for the bus. I don't know what I was thinking about—all that I'd done over the last two years I suppose. Next thing I know, the bus was there and the driver was shouting at me, 'You getting on?'

I shook my head. 'No,' I said, 'I'll wait.' I don't know why I said that or why I just sat there. But then the next bus came along and I got on back to civilian life.

Alun Williams (RAF)

Sometimes, family circumstances forestalled any formal demob process, as Bryn Robbin found out when he went home for a short period of leave:

I only had three months to go when I went home on leave in 1953. I'd been serving in Germany with the BAOR and so I couldn't get home very often. I'd had letters from my mother telling me that dad wasn't well, but when I got home on that last leave I found that he was, in fact, seriously ill. He had a bed in the front room, downstairs, and it was pretty clear that he was actually dying.

I went to his doctor and he told me that he reckoned dad had about two months to live. He was really suffering—'I want to go, boy,' he kept saying. It was terrible for mum, terrible. I told her I wasn't going back to Germany and I said the same to the doctor. 'You've got to go,' he said. I was clear, I didn't care. I wasn't leaving dad dying and my mum alone to cope.

The doctor referred the matter to a solicitor and they consulted with SAFFA, the social care section of the forces. Their advice was to go back. 'You're heading for big trouble,' they told me. I didn't care and I did not go back so, technically, I was AWOL, which was a serious matter. But for two weeks I heard nothing. Then, out of the blue, a compassionate posting came through, to the TA Centre in Port Talbot, just a few miles away.

The job was a doddle. I was the only full-time soldier, the rest were Territorials. I had to go round other TA Centres in the area and talk to the men. I would go to the centre by bus and walk the last few hundred yards. One day, as I got closer, I saw smoke coming from the building—the place had burned down in the night. So I just turned round and went home.

My father died soon after that and then, three weeks later, it was time for my discharge. I had no kit, no uniform, it was all still in Germany. I wasn't accountable to anyone and it was all a bit strange, to say the least, a strange way to finish my national service.

Brinley Robbin (Army)

For some sailors, airmen, and soldiers, their final leave was tinged with humour. There were golden memories and, sometimes, there was also more than a degree of disbelief:

When it came time for my demob, I went to HMS *Drake* to hand back uniforms and things. I went into the Mess Hall for breakfast before I left and I couldn't believe my eyes. There were waiters everywhere, dishing out extra eggs and things to whoever wanted them. And the quality of the food was amazing, all so different from what I'd experienced just two years before when I joined up.

I spoke to the petty officer and he said it was all to do with the running down of national service. They were dealing now with volunteers, men who wanted to be in the Navy, and so they had to be a bit more 'up market' in the food and its delivery. I didn't know whether to laugh or be angry.

Terry Colburn (Navy)

I was formally demobbed at Catterick; that was on the Wednesday. But, on the Thursday, they sent me to Woking to 'say my fond farewells' to the Royal Armoured

Corps. A mate and I took with us a big wooden crate full of light ales, which we kept drinking on the train down. When we got to Woking, there was nowhere for us to sleep so I spent my last night in the Army in the cells. There was nowhere else. The lads in there helped us finish off the light ales—they really enjoyed that.

I was given six weeks' demob leave, complete with pay. So I thought that was great. But the moment I got home, my dad had me running one of his shops straight away—I never did get my leave.

John Gibson (Army)

I was sent back from Africa for my demob at the end of 1948. The memory I'll always carry with me is coming up the Red Sea with the bow wave of the ship gleaming like lights, green neon lights, in the moonlight. It was the phosphorous, but it was quite magical. I had hoped to go up the Suez Canal on the ship, but we were disembarked and sent up by train. We picked up another troop ship at Alexandria.

Back in England, I went up to York for my demob. Then I took the train home. I slept the night on Gloucester station because there was no connection and got home early the next morning.

I'd kept my house key all through national service, all through those lonely days and nights in Africa, and I just let myself in. I hadn't told them I was coming and it was a hell of a shock for the family to hear me in the hallway.

Haydn Burgess (Army)

On leaving the services, almost the first thing conscripts had to do was find a job. Most of them had a few weeks paid leave to tide them over while they were looking for work, but that could only be a temporary situation and the need to make a living was paramount. For some, the services that they had just left offered a way forward, for others it was back to what they knew:

In my final months in the RAF, I'd been attached to the boy entrants school at RAF St Athan, helping with the training young lads (some of them civilians) were getting. It interested me and I thought the training field was something I might like to join.

I started applying for training jobs before I came out of the RAF and was offered the post of apprentice training officer at Aberporth on the Cardigan coast. We trained apprentices from places like Trecwn, Pendine, and Milford Haven. I spent the rest of my working life at Aberporth.

Gerry Evans (RAF)

I had met one fellow on the base in Cyprus; he had been a draughtsman and I thought that sounded interesting—and I could draw. So after a week back home, I called the first engineering company I found in the Glasgow phone book, Babcock and Wilcox in Renfrew, and was promptly offered the position of apprentice draughtsman.

The education officer was ex-RAF and he told me that companies like Babcock were very keen to employ returned servicemen because they were invariably better focused than young lads without the national service experience.

Colin MacCallum (RAF)

I was demobbed on 15 January 1952. Within a fortnight, I was back doing what I knew best, working on the sailing barges along the Thames Estuary and the North Sea coast. But that was hard work, really hard, pulling up sails and anchors, running onto mud banks to discharge cargoes, the work never stopped.

I was on the barges for twelve months after national service, but the work was beginning to fall off. The coal runs stopped and I could see the end coming, the end of barges as a commercial enterprise. So I left the sea. I became a lighthouse keeper for a while, but even that was a changing world as automatic lights were brought in.

John Cotton (Army)

I was demobbed on 6 May 1953, just before the Queen's Coronation. But I had my job all secured long before I left the Army. I was home in Cheltenham on compassionate leave about twelve months before I was due to be demobbed. One of the accountants I knew from before I went into the Army rang me up and asked how long I still had to do. When I told him twelve months, he just said, 'Fine, I'll keep a job open for you.' He did and, within a few days of my demob, I was back in work as if the two-year break had never happened.

Gordon Denley (Army)

Technically, demob was not the end of national service. All soldiers, sailors, and airmen were immediately enrolled in the reserve and, as reservists, were supposed to attend an annual training camp with the Territorials, the Royal Naval Reserve, or the RAF Reserve Section. In fact, many ex-national servicemen were never asked to attend any camp or training exercise. For them, it was as if the reserve status never existed. Others, when they were notified, simply refused to take part in such activities and, with the running down and eventual end of the national service system, there was little that the authorities could do.

Some men were called back, particularly during a crisis such as the Egyptian war and the British and French invasion of Suez in 1956. They were not asked to fight, but acted simply as reserve troops, taking the place of men who had been sent out to problem areas:

I was demobbed in 1951 and went onto the reserve—no choice in the matter, it just happened. I was supposed to go to camp each year for the next couple of years. In fact,

I did it once. I had a week outside Blackpool, then a week at Watchet in Somerset with a Bofers unit, who had their actual base in Aberdeen. I was courting by then, so I was pretty pleased that I was never asked to go again.

Ian Norrie (RAF Regiment)

In the reserve, you were supposed to be ready to be called back if ever there was an emergency. I actually received my 'stand-by' papers to cover the boys who went to Suez, but I was never called up. Perhaps if that particular crisis had gone on a bit longer I might have been recalled. But luckily—for me, anyway because the whole affair was a total mess up, beginning to end—I never had to go back to the Army.

John Gibson (Army)

I went on the first reserve training—'Z' training it was called—that the Army ran. Two weeks on Salisbury Plain.

It was all a bit of a joke. The REME boys, the regulars, didn't want to know us, would hardly let us into their workshops. So we sat in the back of a 3-tonner and told stories and jokes most of the time. The battery sergeant-major, from Bristol, knew more dirty stories than anyone I've ever known.

We were told we wouldn't be allowed off camp at any time during the fortnight, but the battery sergeant-major said I could slip off for the weekend as long as I wasn't on fire picket or guard. He said, 'There's a hole in the fence, use that.' I went through the hole in the netting, walked into the nearest village, and got a lift home for the weekend. I went back by train for the last week.

Arthur Ainger (Army)

On discharge, I was put into the reserve for a period. I guess, unlike the Army, the RNR was still a significant force. Anyway, I gained promotion to lieutenant and was present at the tenth anniversary of the D-Day landings. I was also on ship when we escorted the Queen and the Duke of Edinburgh to Oslo in 1955. So I suppose my period in the reserve wasn't as empty as that of most people.

John Mayer (Navy)

Once I was out of the Navy, I was supposed to be on the reserve for four or five years. But nothing ever happened, nobody ever called me. I think it was like that for a lot of national servicemen.

Geoff Lewis (Navy)

When I was doing my 'Z' or reserve training, there was a bloke from Plymouth with us. He'd been in the Tank Corps for his national service. One night, he just disappeared and was gone four or five days. When he came back, he was driving a tank! Seriously, a tank! He drove it straight into the building, took the pine end clean out. 'You can't leave that there,' we said.

'Yes I can, it's filling the gap.'

It was pretty cold out on Salisbury Plain. Then one of the men said we should burn Blanco. I was amazed at how well the stuff burned. A real glow and plenty of heat. So we sat there, burning Blanco and playing cards.

Arthur Ainger (Army)

For the men who had been called up, national service was a period out of time, two years when their lives were suspended or put into limbo. Friendships were forged in adversity, but they were peculiar to the moment, different in that most of them did not last once the circumstances that had created them were removed. Nearly everyone went away after demob, vowing to keep in touch, but it rarely happened:

When you were demobbed, you left promising to keep in touch with everyone. And to begin with you did—the very least you did was to send Christmas cards. It wasn't so easy then to keep contact like it is today, no mobile phones or things like that. But gradually the Christmas cards stopped coming or you stopped sending them and you lost touch with men who had been bosom buddies during your time in the Navy.

George Moretta (Fleet Air Arm)

I had a great mate in the Army. Ginger and I were together through training and all of our service. We did actually meet up after we were demobbed, but it wasn't the same. Something was missing and so we didn't keep in touch.

Brian Wheeler (Army)

Friendships that had meant the world to servicemen during their two years in the forces usually had little significance once men picked up the threads of their lives again. Within a few years, many of them were married, many bought houses, and, with families to provide for and mortgages to pay, it often seemed that people who had meant so much now actually had very little in common. It was, like facing death and danger, an occupational hazard.

15

End of a System

By the end of the 1950s, it was clear to everyone that national service had outlived its usefulness—if it had ever been really useful to start with. Imposed by the government on the armed forces and on the public in general, almost from the beginning there seemed to be a lack of clarity in much of what the national service recruits were asked to do. As far as the military was concerned, the conscripts were there—and continued to be 'there'—throughout the 1950s. They were a fact of life, but whether they could ever be really useful was another matter altogether:

> As early as 1949 it had become apparent to political and military leaders that the principal of universal liability to national service was a double-edged sword.[1]

The call up was, even in those early years, providing the armed forces with more men than they could easily and usefully absorb. It was also draining resources to provide them with training and accommodation. Perhaps even more importantly, national service removed fit and able young men from the economy of a bankrupt country that desperately needed their involvement.[2]

There were continued rumblings for most of the 1950s. Writers like Alan Sillitoe, Arnold Wesker, and David Lodge all produced satirical novels and plays, lampooning the national service process. The 1958 film *Carry on Sergeant* (much more than simply the first in a long line of successful British comedy films) took the satirical approach to a new level, displaying the ridiculousness of the system—the bullying NCOs and the mindless activities designed simply to keep recruits busy—to a wide and totally incredulous audience.

Throughout the period when people were questioning the validity of national service, Prime Minister Harold MacMillan declared that the populace of Britain had 'never had it so good'. It was an attitude or a stance that grew to new heights with the debacle of the Suez Crisis, when Britain and France were forced to a humiliating climb down over their military reaction to President Nasser's nationalisation of the Suez Canal.

A 1957 White Paper from the Ministry of Defence was clear. There needed to be a new way of planning, new strategic thinking, if Britain's military commitments in the future were to become in any way effective. In a nuclear age, it was obvious to military planners and to government officials that the country no longer required a large, standing Army or a massive RAF and Navy. Therefore, given the climate, what use was there in calling up young men for a period of military service?

For several years, the Army and RAF in particular had been almost at a loss over how to employ its conscripts. There simply was not enough work for them to do. One late recruit, Stan Richards, actually lived at home during his stint of national service. His family home was a few miles away from his camp and he walked to the telephone kiosk and phoned in each morning to see if there was a parade or some work to do. He generally operated a three-day week.[3] It was a far cry from the early days of bull and Blanco.

By the late 1950s, most of Britain's colonial possessions had gone or were in the process of being given their independence. The country had a commitment to NATO and its allies, but it was already a junior partner as far as the US was concerned. Thousands of young, barely trained infantrymen were clearly not what the Army needed.

Quite apart from the practicalities of the situation, there was also the moral issue. Did compulsory military service do more harm than good? It was a difficult question to answer.

The serial criminal Harry Roberts, later convicted of shooting and killing three policemen, fought the Mau-Mau in Kenya and Communist terrorists in Malaya. He felt no remorse in shooting his military enemies, just as he felt no regret when he killed the policemen. He enjoyed his period of national service:

> I didn't find it too difficult. On the contrary, I found the Army quite easy. So did many of the Borstal Boys. We seemed to get on a lot better than the ordinary civilians who were called up. Army life agreed with me. I loved the discipline.[4]

Whether Roberts would have graduated to a life of crime without the brutalising nature of Army life is one of the great imponderables. Like the Kray twins, however, he left the Army and went on to another profession where the use of guns was acceptable.

Using Roberts and the Krays as yardsticks is dangerous. There were thousands of others who passed through the Army and the other services, who fought in places like Malaya and Korea, and did not become brutalised or turn to crime. At the end of the day, it all depended on the individual, his psychological make-up, and the society in which he had spent his formative years.

The debates dragged on, but the decision had been made by 1960. National service would end in the spring of 1963. The last national serviceman was Private Fred Turner, who was discharged on 7 May that year. The last national service officer was Lieutenant Richard Vaughan, who left the Army Pay Corps on 13 May 1963. Adolescents and young men who had been preparing to do their time—perhaps looking forward to it with trepidation, even fear—were undoubtedly glad to see it go. Men who actually served in one of the armed forces had a rather different perspective:

I was quite happy in the RAF. I don't think the idea of enjoyment ever came into it. There was a job to be done, you just got on and did it. I don't think national service did me any harm. I was well fed and entertained and there was a sense of achievement in the job. All in all, I would say that the RAF looked after me pretty well during my two years of service.

Michael Beddis (RAF)

I enjoyed my time in the Navy very much and looking back now I'm glad that I did it. But when the time came to leave the Navy I was glad to go—I'd had two Christmases away from home, and a birthday, and I wanted to celebrate with my family. I think, more than anything, those two years in the Navy taught me what home really is. For that alone I'll always be grateful.

Jim Clarke (Navy)

I wouldn't have missed the Army for anything. Even though, as a merchant seaman, I could have easily got out of it. I was happy to do my time. And now I'm so glad I did. It taught me discipline and self-reliance.

John Cotton (Army)

National service was a unique social experiment, although its originators would hardly have seen it in that light. It has to be viewed in the context of the time, in a virtually bankrupt, post-war Britain that still retained huge commitments across the world. The threat of further conflict was ever-present and young conscripts were as important in maintaining Britain's place in the world as their Second World War counterparts had been a few years earlier.

National service and the presence of thousands of young conscripts did not stop wars erupting across the globe. If anything, it was only the presence of nuclear weapons and the threat of an atomic attack that kept the world relatively peaceful so that conflict, when it came, was localised. The conscripts were never the answer to the problem, but they did try to bridge the gap, to hold the fort.

All national servicemen have their stories. Time and experience may have caused a degree of embellishment, but the main thing that comes through from every man who served in the Army, Navy, or RAF is a simple statement: 'I'm glad I did it.'

The one word that all national servicemen use more than any other is 'comradeship'. Those two years in the armed forces—two years at a key moment in their lives, at the end of adolescence and at the beginning of manhood—gave them friendships that sustained and helped them through many difficult moments. They were friendships that were destined not to last beyond the confines of the national service period (perhaps they were too intense and too specific in their purpose for that), but, at the time, comradeship was what got men through:

I made some wonderful friends during my time in the RAF, wonderful. I always say that the best definition of friendship is one I picked up during my service life—a friend is someone who shares a cup of tea with you when neither of you has any money. To me that sums up my time as a national serviceman.

John Williams (RAF Regiment)

Endnotes

Chapter 1

1. Hart, R. A., *Above and Beyond the Call*
2. *The Western Mail*, 15 February 1947
3. *Ibid.*, 27 January 1947
4. *Ibid.*, 7 May 1947
5. Hennessy, P., *Never Again*, p. 438
6. *Astral*, Summer 2012
7. 'Post War: A North East Perspective', www.rememberingscotlandatwar.org.uk/Accessible/Exhibition/129/National-Service-
8. Lodge, D., 'Afterword' in *Ginger, You're Barmy*
9. Sandbrook, D., *White Heat*, p. 200
10. Hickman, T., *The Call Up*, p. 28
11. Lodge, D., p. 95
12. Thomas, L., *The Virgin Soldiers*, p. 193

Chapter 2

1. Lodge, D., *Ginger, You're Barmy*, p. 12
2. Priest, D., 'The Peacetime Conscripts', www.bbc.co.uk/history/british/modern/peacetime_conscripts_01.shtml

Chapter 3

1. Priest, D., 'The Peacetime Conscripts', www.bbc.co.uk/history/british/modern/peacetime_conscripts_01.shtml
2. Doyle, P., and Evans, P., *National Service*, p. 23
3. Abse, D., *Goodbye Twentieth Century*, p. 123

Chapter 6

1. Hickman, T., *The Call Up*, p. 142

Chapter 8

1. Emsley, C., *Soldier, Sailor, Beggarman, Thief*, p. 142

Chapter 9

1. Hickman, T., *The Call Up*, p. 141

Chapter 10

1. 'Post War: A North East Perspective', www.rememberingscotlandatwar.org.uk/Accessible/Exhibition/129/National-Service-

Chapter 11

1. Hennesey, P., *Having it So Good*
2. *Hansard*, 5 July 1955
3. Smith, L., *Voices Against War*
4. 'Conscription in the UK', Wikipedia, en.wikipedia.org/wiki/Conscription_in_the_United_Kingdom
5. *Hansard*, 15 November 1951

Chapter 12

1. *Hansard*, 5 July 1955

Chapter 14

1. Hickman, T., *The Call Up*, p. 275

Chapter 15

1. Priest, D., 'The Peacetime Conscripts', www.bbc.co.uk/history/british/modern/peacetime_conscripts_01.shtml
2. *Ibid.*
3. Shindler, C., *National Service*, pp. 263–265
4. Emsley, C., *Soldier, Sailor, Beggarman, Thief*, p. 191

Bibliography

Books

Abse, D., *Goodbye Twentieth Century*, (London: Pimlico, 2003)
Carradice, P., *Coming Home: Wales After the War*, (Llandysul: Gomer, 2005)
Doyle, P., and Evans, P., *National Service*, (Oxford: Shire, 2012)
Emsley, C., *Soldier, Sailor, Beggarman, Thief*, (Oxford: OUP, 2013)
Hennesey, P., *Never Again*, (London: Vintage, 1993)
Hewison, R., *Under Siege*, (London: Weidenfeld and Nicolson, 1977)
Lloyd, S., *Suez*, (London: Jonathan Cape, 1978)
Lodge, D., *Ginger, You're Barmy*, (London: Vintage, 2011)
Sainsbury, A. B., and Phillips, F. L., *The Royal Navy Day by Day*, (Stroud: Sutton Publishing, 2005)
Sandbrook, D., *White Heat*, (London: Little Brown, 2006)
Shindler, C., *National Service*, (London: Sphere, 2012)
Smith, L., *Voices Against War: A Century of Protest*, (Edinburgh: Mainstream Publishing, 2010)
Stephens, M., *My Shoulder to the Wheel*, (Talybont: Y Lolfa, 2015)
Thomas, L., *The Virgin Soldiers*, (London: Arrow Books, 2005)
Thorne, T., *Brasso, Blanco and Bull*, (London: Constable, 2012)
Vinen, R., *National Service*, (London: Allen Lane, 2014)
Ward, H., *World Powers in the Twentieth Century*, (London: BBC/Heinemann, 1978)
Wesker, A., *Chips with Everything*, (London: Jonathan Cape, 1962)
Williams, H., *A Severe Case of Dandruff*, (Llandysul: Gomer, 1999)
Woodman, R., *Voyage East*, (London: John Murray, 1988)

Magazines, Newspapers, and Reports

Astral (National Service RAF Association)
Hansard, 15 November 1951 and 5 July 1955
Hart, R. A., *Above and Beyond the Call*, (University of Stirling Thesis, 2009)
Miscellany 17 (Pentyrch and District Local History Society)
Sea Breezes
Siegfried's Journal
The Star, 26 October 1951
The Western Mail (various dates)

Websites

BBC History Blog (www.bbc.co.uk/history/british/modern/peacetime_conscripts_01.shtml)
  'Conscription in the United Kingdom', Wikipedia, en.wikipedia.org/wiki/Conscription_in_the_
  United_Kingdom
'Post War: A North East Perspective', www.rememberingscotlandatwar.org.uk/Accessible/
  Exhibition/129/National-Service-